Carolina Evangelical Divinity School Library

Pastor Preacher Person

DEVELOPING A PASTORAL MINISTRY IN DEPTH

David K. Switzer

ABINGDON
Nashville

PASTOR, PREACHER, PERSON:
DEVELOPING A PASTORAL MINISTRY IN DEPTH

Copyright © 1979 by Abingdon

All rights reserved.
No part of this book may be reproduced in any manner whatsoever without written permission of the publisher except brief quotations embodied in critical articles or reviews. For information address Abingdon, Nashville, Tennessee

Library of Congress Cataloging in Publication Data

SWITZER, DAVID K. 1925-
Pastor, preacher, person.
1. Clergy—Office. 2. Pastoral theology. I. Title.
BV660.2.S88 253 78-24018

ISBN 0-687-30137-8

MANUFACTURED BY THE PARTHENON PRESS AT
NASHVILLE, TENNESSEE, UNITED STATES OF AMERICA

Preface

I have always been primarily interested in and committed to the local parish ministry. This may appear to be a peculiar or even incomprehensible statement, coming as it does from one whose post-seminary ministry has included a total of only eight years in three local congregations in contrast with nine years as a college chaplain and now eleven years at a theological seminary. But the chaplaincy methodology was based upon a congregational model, including weekly preaching, and a primary motivation for going to the seminary was to try to bring to bear upon theological education at this place my conviction that the local parish is definitely where most of the action is and to attempt to utilize my knowledge of local congregational life to shape the best possible seminary education for leadership in the church. Finally, my commitment to preaching has led to my being a "Sunday Chaplain" at Timberlawn Psychiatric Hospital in Dallas, where I have been preaching regularly for five years.

It is out of this concern for the ministry of the church, particularly, although not exclusively the local parish, and out of my own life and my pastoral care and preaching activities that this book has come. It is my sincere hope and prayer that it will play its role in our continuing to grow as persons and as ministerial professionals.

It should, of course, be pointed out that the book has some of its own earlier written sources. Chapter 1 has appeared in somewhat briefer form as an article entitled "The Minister as Pastor and Person" in the fall 1975 issue of *Pastoral Psychology.* Chapters 3 and 4 appeared in very brief form as an article, "Door de prediking inspelen op menselijke behoeften" in *praktische theologie,* a Dutch journal of practical theology, the 1977 issue, no. 5. Both of these journals have graciously given permission for the material to be used in this new form and context.

I wish to express my gratitude to Jerry Lewis, M.D., Director of the Timberlawn Foundation for Psychiatric Education and Research, for allowing me the use of a very comfortable and quiet office in the foundation facilities, where most of this writing was done, and without which it may very well have not been accomplished.

I want to express my deep appreciation once more to Gladys Mollet who has had the unenviable experience of typing this material several times. Such discipline and patience and good spirit must surely have its reward, although, heaven knows, it is not a monetary one at the present time.

Contents

To my parents
Horace S. and Helen Kone Switzer
in appreciation for their deep love,
wisdom, and Christian faith

and

to Joe Z and Beryl Goodwin Tower
Pastor, friends, "parents in the ministry"

all of whom contributed essentially to
my becoming a minister of the church

Introduction

Toward a Theology and Practice of Being a Minister

It is no sin to be properly concerned about ourselves, and most of us ministers are. We think about ourselves as persons, how we handle our own feelings and behavior. We give attention to our families, work on these relationships, and often feel guilty about not being better husbands or wives, fathers or mothers. Or, if single, how we think of ourselves as unmarried ministers and the peculiar issues related to this state (and status) are related to the quality of our lives and ministry. Our sense of being prepared for ministry and our evaluation of our competence is a part of our comfort or discomfort within ourselves as we go about our work and reflect on it.

Are there systematic ways of dealing with ourselves as persons, pastors, and professionals that can assist us toward a sense of wholeness as we live and function with ministry as our vocation? To what should we be attentive as we seek to improve the quality of our lives and the competence of our ministry?

We are also concerned about the church within which we work: the worldwide Church of Christ, if we are not to be provincial Christians (actually a contradiction in terms); the denomination to which we belong, if we are to have a clearer sense of identity and if we are to be assisted in our effectiveness; the congregations of our city or geographical area, of whatever denomination, if we are to have the greatest experience of the co-ordinated impact of our mutual ministry on a definable local population; but also of necessity, and quite appropriately so, our own particular congregation. It is here that our greatest energies are expended, the worshipping community toward which most of our thought is directed, out of which we minister to the larger community, and within which our energies as persons and professionals must primarily be renewed, else we will become frustrated, exhausted, and ineffective. The quality of life of *this* congregation is the central focus of our ministry, the building up of the body of Christ *here.* The quality of the life of this local community of faith is the most powerful outcome of our efforts in terms of unambiguous witness to the larger community and gives rise to social and evangelistic outreach which is credible and persuasive to those beyond our congregation. Yet how is this quality of life concretely defined and evaluated? Love, yes. But to what behavior does love refer as we work together as a congregation? Where do we get our definitions and descriptions?

Among the functions of the ministry most closely related to the edifying (building up) of the church—the establishing and maintaining of a high quality of congregational life—are preaching, education, administration, and pastoral care which have those qualities which empower human transformation. We ministers are all deeply concerned about these functions which we are called to perform, and to which we must bring active leadership. How do we understand these functions? How can we become more effective?

This book is for all of us who have these concerns. It does not seek to discuss each of these subjects systematically, or in detail. But it does make some concrete suggestions about the church, its ministers, and its ministry, and it is hoped does so in a way that will raise further questions and stimulate ministers to further investigation of themselves, their congregations, their style and competence.

Naturally, something ought to hold a book together besides its binding. Any serious attempt to make a contribution to the life of a person or to the community of faith on the part of a minister writing to ministers (or any Christian writing to Christians or sincere seekers) may be united in a variety of ways. This may be a single *subject,* approached from several directions and elaborated systematically and in detail, or it may be a *collection of topics* within a broader field. Quite a different focus is that of the illustration of a particular *method* of handling material.

It is into this last category that this volume whose content is the minister and ministry seems to fall. It is not primarily a systematic exploration of the minister as a person and a professional, nor of the church, nor how to do the functions of ministry, although as has already been stated, these *are* our genuine concerns and the book discusses these.

Rather this single volume can be seen as relatively comprehensive only in the sense that the areas of the minister-church-functions of ministry define the main outer limits within which the method is applied. Actually, far more is *not* said about each of these subjects than is attempted. While it is hoped that the "content" discussion of each of them will be useful, a greater contribution might possibly be made if the reader will pay attention to the methodology of developing the content.

The particular method which is followed in this book is that of adapting some of the insights and procedures and research data of psychotherapy to ministers' ways of thinking about themselves, their operational context within the church, and two central ministerial functions—preaching and pastoral care. As the particular psychotherapeutic material is introduced, a biblical/theological rationale for doing so is discussed and references made to the way in which the contemporary materials support and are supported by certain biblical/theological approaches. The outcome is hopefully a specific contribution to the present life of the minister and his/her function of preaching and pastoral care, and to the life of the local congregation. Finally, in a brief epilogue, this method itself as an exercise in practical theology will be discussed in somewhat more detail.

I. The Minister: Person, Pastor, Professional

I was sitting in a meeting of a living unit at a psychiatric hospital recently and some of the residents of that division were voicing their uneasiness and anger at the number of students who came in, observed for a while, then left, without ever becoming fully a part of the life of the people there. One of the patients said with considerable feeling, "It's like being in a circus!" Several others picked up on this image, all in the sense that they were a part of the *act,* a show for which they had not originally volunteered, but now for which they are compelled to perform so that others might observe. Anxiety, anger, resistance: all quite understandable.

But there I sat. What role did I play in this circus? Certainly I did not see myself as a spectator, but rather as a participant in the show itself. But in what way? What *is* the minister's act in this circus? Inevitably my mind turned to Faber's analogy of the minister as a clown.[1] A clown? Surely not! We are not comics in the drama of life! We take very seriously the high nature of our vocation as response to God, participating in the life of God himself as we seek to respond to, and exemplify in the concrete functions of our ministry, the "being-for-others" of Christ.

Yet, examined seriously, this is an image which leads to a deeper exploration of what it means to *be* a minister and some of what is involved in the development of the minister as a person and a professional, leading to greater competence in the functions of ministry and greater fulfillment as a human being. Important contributions are offered to both self-understanding as minister-person and minister-doer by research designed to improve operational competence in psychotherapy.

It does not usually occur to most of us to think of ourselves as clowns, although if we have any objective view of ourselves at all, there must be occasions when we laugh at ourselves and our behavior. However, those who have read Faber's book are aware of something of the earnestness of purpose and depth of meaning in the comparison. Those who have not may possibly be shocked and offended by the use of the clown image as an appropriate one for ministers. However, I would like for the reader to withhold final judgment until we have the opportunity to expand the image in the context of the pastoral functions of ministry. With regard specifically to the ordained minister, there seem to be at least three elements comprising the term "pastor": (a) our awareness of ourselves as persons who are serving God as we help others, (b) how others respond to us when they see us as ministers, including their responses both at conscious and unconscious levels, and (c) the connotation that we are fully professionals, with all of what that word means as it is commonly applied to *all* professional fields.

There is an interrelationship between the person and role of the minister in his/her functioning as pastor. Therefore, it seems possible to weave insights derived from the life of a clown and the elements of the term pastor into a discussion which may help us better understand ourselves as persons and our role and functioning as pastors, and thereby lead to a greater sense of self and perhaps to more effective work.

To me there are several characteristics of a clown which can form a framework for the minister's self-understanding as a person and a professional:

1. The clown is not only the genuinely human thread that runs through the entire circus, holding it together as a coherent and meaningful process rather than just a series of unrelated, flawless, expert acts, but also brings to bear upon these other acts a perspective that enables us to see beyond the present moment.

2. The clown represents the depth and breadth of humanity, the point of contact with the gamut of emotions experienced by the people in the audience, providing a point of identification that we do not easily have with the "expert technicians," such as the trapeze and high wire artists, the animal trainers, and the riders.

3. Yet the clown does this as a highly trained, competent professional whose professional acts grow out of his/her own humanity and his/her understanding of the humanity of others.

4. Finally, the effectiveness of the pastor as professional is never separated from his/her own being as a person.

The Minister: Humanizer

First, the clown is both the genuinely human thread that holds the circus together as a whole process and the one who brings to bear upon the here and now a deeper and farther-reaching perspective out of which to view this present.

The need in our world is for far more than a series of well-performed technical/physical acts. The hospital as the context of pastoral functioning provides a vivid illustration of this point because of the critical sharpness with which the immediate personal issues are drawn. A few other settings of ministry have something of the same life-death urgency about them, but the typical minister is much less often involved. Many other aspects of our society's life continually call for ministry, and we occasionally can find ways of responding, but the sense of critical immediacy is usually far less.

In the hospital, a place where we constantly go, the need of persons is for something in addition to the technical knowledge and skills of the various medical personnel as these converge in a series of expert acts (diagnosis, operative procedures, medication, physical care), although obviously these comprise central events in the process, and a superior degree of competence is necessary in them. With all of that, the hospital is the scene of a total human drama, with different acts and different outcomes, and in which all human emotions are drawn out with intensity. It is a place where the meaning of human existence is both challenged and confirmed. Who deals with all of this as his/her *primary* function? The surgeon, the nurse, the hospital administrator? No! Rather, it is the minister. The call in the hospital is for a response to the *total humanity* of persons, which includes some recognition of the divine dimensions of human life, as persons struggle with the issues of their own life and death and the meaning of it all, and as they seek a perspective not brought to them by the basic medical skills of the others about them. Their desperate need is for someone to help them put it all together in some sort of meaningful whole. There is obviously more than one way to go about doing this, but a very significant assistance is given by the presence and functions of a person of faith, operating self-consciously out of the context of faith, with faith sensitizing his/her responsiveness as a human being, motivating his/her commitment to the patient and members of the family, and undergirding his/her professional competence.

Other areas of life are in desperate need of the same sensitization, humanization, larger perspective, coherence, and wholeness: business, finance, politics and government, international relations, educational systems, the criminal justice system, urban development, and others. These are extremely difficult areas for us ministers to find opportunities and methods with which to intervene with any sense of effectiveness. Most of us are aware of our sense of helplessness and frustration in our usual inability to respond effectively to the magnitude and complexity of these needs. But whether we are attempting to intervene in these areas or in the smaller institutions of society and in our own church and community, we pastors bring in ourselves the human dimension which is necessary to the personal relationships that are always the arena of our work, and we bring the divine dimension in our own faith and our chosen profession, and these are always one.

As ministers, our faith is an integral part of our personhood and our profession. Our faith is that which is constantly telling us who we are as children of God, assisting the quality of self-acceptance that both pushes and allows us to continue to come more fully in touch with every aspect of our being, that finds its expression in our personal relationships in ways appropriate to person and situation, that facilitates our openness in the sharing of our own humanness. It brings a meaningful perspective to our fragile and tenuous lives in this world, so accentuated in the hospital, at the time of death, in individual and family crisis, and in other situations where in some sense our lives or the meaning of our lives are at stake.

But our faith is also tied in with our professional life. However our faith in God may be articulated in words, most ministers have entered their profession because of the impetus of that faith in the direction of the full living out of its expression and, for a high percentage of ministers, this is the motivation for continuing in the profession. This is not to suggest, of course, that the reason we stay in is experienced and stated in precisely the same form as when we made our first decision or decisions. This would be no more true than to declare that we stay married for exactly the same reason that we got married in the first place, or that a person remains in psychotherapy for the identical conscious motivation that he/she had in initiating the process, but that in some way, in some set of terms that make sense to us, our functioning as ministers is related to an awareness of the meaning of God in human life within the context of the community of faith, and that our acts of ministry, although truly *ours* as persons, are also acts representative of God and his community of persons.

Ministerial Identity

In my experience, Erikson is quite correct in placing a central focus on "occupational identity" as being crucial in the total identity development of the adolescent male[2] (and, perhaps, increasingly, of the adolescent female). Not only is the "occupational identity" the initial expression of the needs and drives that are beginning to come together in the adolescent's struggle for selfhood, it also becomes a dynamic center which then draws loose forces within the personality together and channels them in particular directions in powerful ways. Occupation continues to share a central place in the selfhood of most persons over the years. It becomes increasingly an integral part of an individual's self-image, and for a majority an occupational crisis is also a crisis of selfhood. Most ministers not only *work* at their profession, and invest time and energy, but at the core of the self is "minister," a bound collection of self-images, values, faith, and commitments—a person who has responded and *is responding* to a vocation, not just one who has chosen an occupation. I do not just *perform* a ministry, I *am* a minister. This is the way I think of myself, and on most occasions I act out of this awareness of my personhood.

The Minister as a Symbol

Finally, we ministers are not only who *we* understand we are as persons and as pastors, but we are the ones whom others see and respond to in particular ways when they become aware that we are ordained clergy.[3] This response has some elements that may be quite conscious, but these are always combined with those that are unconcious. With any person or family or group with whom we are engaged as pastor, we bring not only the power of a personal presence but also our impact as symbols. Every professional who has clients is not only who he/she is but also what the other person perceives him/her to be, and the source of much of the strength of these feelings is a part of the person's unconscious processes. We are not only persons, we are also symbols.

Tillich lists a number of characteristics of symbols in the context of his declaration that "man's ultimate concern must be expressed symbolically, because symbol alone is able to express the ultimate."[4] The first characteristic is the most obvious one, that a symbol points beyond itself to something else. However, second, unlike a simple sign, a symbol participates in that to which it points. There is somehow a direct inseparable relationship between the two. The third characteristic of symbol is that it opens up levels of reality that otherwise are closed for us. And fourth, it also unlocks dimensions and elements of our inner being, which correspond to the dimensions and elements of reality. What Tillich seems to be expressing here without using his sort of language is that as a result of the symbol's participation in the reality to which it points, it also has the power to communicate something of that reality to the person for whom the symbol is meaningful.[5]

The ordained minister must be aware that he/she is a symbol of the reality that underlies the meaningfulness of Christian faith if he/she is going to function at the highest level of effectiveness in relationships with others. In other words, quite apart from one's own being as a person, the pastor is perceived by others as being the physical representation to the community of faith and, at least to some extent to the larger community, of the reality of God. The very physical presence of the minister has the power to stimulate those internal images, which through early learning in a highly emotionally charged relationship of dependence, have become a part of an individual's intrapersonal dynamics. These primitive images are a part of that individual's internal resources and are strong unconscious forces affecting every aspect of his/her life.

The identification of these unconscious forces, their strength, and their constant influencing of our perceptions of one another and our relationships, is a major contribution of psychotherapy to us as ministers, both in terms of our self-knowledge and of the need to consider their reality in our interaction with others.

Now, to be sure, it must be recognized that in the development of quite a number of people these images have negative forces attached to them, but even in many of these, as well as in a large number of other people who have been related to a religious community, they are positive. The minister is a physical representation of the whole community of faith, of the tradition, of a way of viewing the meaning of life, of the dynamic power of faith, and of God Himself. This is a significant factor not to be overlooked when the pastor visits the sick or grief-stricken or engages in counseling or intervenes in crisis or performs any other professional ministerial function. Because of this symbol-power, there may be unconscious negative forces to be dealt with, worked through, and overcome, as well as unconscious positive forces that actually become available to many persons in a strengthening and healing way during their time of distress, or in a guiding and supporting way at times of critical decision. While other mental health professionals are also symbols, because of the long-term history of religious communities, the relationship between religion and culture, and the total exposure of many persons to the religious community as children, its collection of symbols, its ritual, and its ministry, and the way in which this exposure is integrally tied into the nuclear family itself, the symbol of the pastor seems to be of a different order in terms of its strength.

To summarize, the first major point is that the minister has a unique role to play in the world in terms of humanizing the total series of acts and events in business and commerce, in medicine and law, in all forms of work and human transactions, and, in so doing, has the potential of weaving a thread of meaning that has the power to transform these acts into a coherent process in the experience of the person and other related individuals, bringing to bear upon the present moment a perspective that penetrates beyond the present moment, a perspective that, in some sense, brings the "not yet" into the "now," the future into the present. The minister does this by simply presenting him/herself as a *person,* as a person of *faith,* an expression of which is also his/her *vocation,* and by being aware of and utilizing the responses of the other persons to him/her as a symbol.

Facilitator of Growth

The second point is simply a deepening of one aspect of the first. The clown represents the depth and breadth of humanity so powerfully to us that in a way not accomplished by the "expert technicians" we are enabled to become more aware of who we are, what our real feelings and inner reactions are, and how we appear to others. This initiates a process of growth in us.

The key question for the minister is whether in order to help a person it is sufficient merely to be ordained,to present ourselves as such, and have certain things that we do, or in the absence of specified functions, just to be there. Certainly there are indications that perhaps in some number of instances this may be of some significant help. Our bringing our bodies to a bedside or to a home or an office or to some other place does present the person and the family with what may be for them a powerful symbol, and this may in itself elicit some response, activating deep resources of strength in the form of feelings of safety or security, the diminishing of anxiety, and a sense of peace. If the minister and the person in need are from a faith group in which the efficacy of the Sacraments is emphasized, then the performing of these acts furnishes other symbols that relate the person to the reality of God and that are supportive or even healing.

However, many persons do not have this background and therefore will not be responsive in this way, and the main symbol many of us have to present is simply ourselves. But in either case, what is it that we *then* have that is important to the human life before us? The answer is, as just suggested, ourselves, a certain quality of personhood, the communication of which within relationships has the power to facilitate the catharsis of emotions that exacerbate illness, to stimulate insight, and to develop ego strength.

The Pastor as Professional

A psychologist who has worked in a hospital setting was commenting on the fact that in the sick room it often seems as if the minister is the only person who does not seem to have anything to do, and sometimes we have that feeling about ourselves, as Faber has pointed out, of "feeling like an amateur among acknowledged experts."[6] The psychologist hastened to say that perhaps it is a good thing we do not have a required list of specified functions. He went on to speak of what he perceived to be the value of "unhurried care."

This unhurried care is the personal element, and it is needed in many situations, but it is necessary to keep in mind that it makes a lot of difference who is doing the caring, what sort of person, and how he/she is capable of communicating his/her own personhood.

Evidence derived from research into psychotherapy seems to be preponderantly in contradiction to the idea that just any sort of person may learn certain ideas and techniques and thereby become an effective counselor of others and, by implication, pastor to others. The hypothesis that has been tested, and so far upheld, is that "all effective interpersonal processes share a common core of conditions conducive to facilitative human experiences,"[7] namely, accurate empathy, respect, concreteness, genuineness, self-disclosure, confrontation, and immediacy. These will be defined in a later chapter and their relevance to preaching discussed.

The point here is that these conditions are not just something that we do but are reflections of who we are. A rather obvious fact is that the helping person is a key ingredient in the process in that he/she offers a model of a person who is living effectively. There are crucial elements in the relationship necessary for the growth of persons in distress that the pastor cannot simply produce by something he/she does, unless somehow that is what he/she is, and unless the behavior in the relationship is an authentic expression of his/her own being.[8] The ends and the means of the helping process are the same. We cannot somehow lead a person to where we are not.

Carkhuff refers to the three R's of helping, which are appropriate to discuss in the context of the minister's encounters with persons in distress: (a) the *right* of the helper to intervene in the life of another, (b) the *responsibility* of the helper once intervention has taken place, and (c) the *role* the helper must assume in helping another individual, and, at the same time, the various role conflicts encountered in attempting to implement the responsibilities implied by intervention.[9]

We ministers have not too often questioned our *right* to enter into the lives of other persons in a variety of ways, both by invitation and at our own initiative. Somehow we have assumed this right as proper and inherent in our being ministers. Carkhuff, however, basing his conclusions on a growing body of research data, states that this right must be based on our ability to help, not just on our traditional role. This means that we must be functioning at higher levels of effectiveness ourselves in the relevant areas of concern. "Only the person who is alive and growing can enable the struggling person to choose life at the life and death crisis points."[10] We clergy must not be in the ministry or in counseling work *primarily* to fulfill in these rather temporary pastoral care and counseling relationships those needs of our own that are quite unfulfilled in large areas of our own personal lives, or to find intimacy that we know in no other place. Otherwise, we may end up helping neither ourselves nor others. This, of course, does not deny that in the performance of our ministry, certain important needs of ours are in fact met. It would be self-defeating to be in *any* work where personal needs do not find some fulfillment.

The matter of *responsibility* follows hard on the heels of this statement. If we intervene in the life of another person primarily out of a lack of fulfillment in our own lives, we inevitably act in a distorted manner that is a reflection of this incompleteness. Thus, procedures in relating to the other, and especially in the process of counseling and pastoral care, will be more designed to serve us than to serve the person who is seeking help or whom we visit. The tendency will be to subtract from the responses of the person in need far more than to add, thereby increasing the other person's distortions rather than reducing them. This speaks of responsibility, ours initially to ourselves in regard to our own growth, health, and meaningful relationships, *in order that* we may have something, mainly ourselves, to offer to the others.

The matter of *role* is a particularly important issue for us ministers, for we have a long history, even a tradition, that tells us and the larger society something about who the clergyperson is. Without going into detail here, we need to clarify the difference between what certain of our functions as clergy are, and who it is we really are as individual human beings. We need to be able to utilize the symbolic power of our role, but without hiding behind it or exploiting people with it. Our *role responsibility* as pastors is a commitment to do all that we can that can be translated into benefits for the person who needs help, whatever the nature of that need. Our movement in the process is always from *role* at first to *person* later, a personal relationship "in which neither person allows himself or the other to be less than he can be."[11]

All of this leads to an obvious conclusion. Every pastor must continue to grow as a person in order to increase in effectiveness as a pastor. One of the central functions of the minister is to provide for others a model of a person who experiences some sense of meaning in life, who has a purpose that energizes him/her, who has satisfying relationships, and who is able to apply personal insights through appropriate action. Once having made a decision to be a minister, we no longer have a choice as to whether we will or will not be involved with persons in distress, pain, crisis, or sorrow, as well as other types of pastoral situations. The only choice within this vocational context is how well we are going to function for the other's benefit. The obligation is laid upon us to grow constantly in the direction of being that kind of person who contributes more to the helping process than we take away from it.

Carkhuff summarizes it succinctly:

> Perhaps the point on which to conclude a consideration of the counselor's contribution to helping processes is the point at which all effective helping begins, that is, with an integrated and growing person, one who is personally productive and creative, one whose life is dominated by personal meaning and fulfillment. Without such persons in the helping role there is no hope in the world or for the world.[12]

The Expert Amateur

This focus on the person of the pastor, however, leads us to the last major point. Concerning the clown, it was expressed that his/her deep sense of the strengths and weaknesses of persons and his/her ability to touch our particular strengths and weaknesses in such a way as to assist our own insight and growth are communicated in forms that grow out of serious training and disciplined experience for which the term professional is quite appropriate. The one who appears to be the amateur is in fact an expert in communicating his/her humanity, which in the case of the minister, if we are to be genuine, includes the faith that truly vitalizes our personhood. Communication is our major instrument, the vehicle which carries that which is helpful: healing, sustaining, guiding, and reconciling, to use the four major functions of pastoral care as they are presented by Clebsch and Jaekle.[13]

Our growth as persons, then, our growth in faith, and our growth in our ability to evaluate persons and their situations and to engage with them in a developing relationship in which we are capable both of utilizing in a disciplined manner the most effective forms of communicating ourselves and eliciting their communication of themselves, as well as within the context of our personhood and discipline being able to improvise to the benefit of the other person—*all* of this is our profession. It is in *all* of this that we need to be trained and guided and continue to grow. If this is done, we are genuine professionals.

The interesting thing, though, is that while in the midst of the other specialists we may sometimes appear to be amateurs, and may even feel so ourselves, we need not feel apologetic for our existence and presence. It is useful to be reminded that the word amateur in its original meaning need not conflict with the concept of professional at all, but should properly be caught up into it. Amateur comes from the Latin *amator,* the lover, someone who does something because he/she loves it. There must be some of this in *any* professional, and most certainly there should be a large element of "the lover" in the pastor.

Our professional status (and professional literally means one who acknowledges something about him/herself before others and, in our sense here, that he/she is competent) is determined by the *competence* with which our loving is done, not just the degree to which we love. The implications of this statement are insitutionalized in our society by certain characteristics of what we call the professions.

Glasse, in his book, *Profession: Minister,* proposes that

> a professional is identified by five characteristics: (1) He is an *educated* man, master of some body of knowledge . . . (2) He is an *expert man,* master of some specific cluster of skills. These skills while requiring some talent, can be learned and sharpened by practice under supervision. (3) He is an *institutional man,* relating himself to society and rendering his service through a historical social institution of which he is partly servant, partly master . . . (4) He is a *responsible man* who professes to be able to act competently in situations which require his services. He is committed to practice his profession according to high standards of competence and ethics. Finally, (5) he is a *dedicated man.*[14]

We may well wish that he had not used such exclusively male language, but he has clearly defined for us the direction of our tasks if we are to be truly professional in ministry, and he has presented an outline which suggests to us a commitment to an ever-increasing level of competence in that which we do, summarized here as:

1. Our ability to evaluate persons and their situations, what it is they need, directions in which they need to grow.
2. Our discipline in communicating ourselves and eliciting their communication of themselves at such a level of effectiveness that they are sustained, guided, reconciled, healed (the last including, obviously, the healing of emotional life, of spirit, of relationships even in one whose body in fact may not be healed.)
3. Out of our competence in evaluation and discipline in communication, the ability to do that which is original and creative within the interaction of a given situation.
4. All of these three presuppose the quality of the personhood of the pastor.

Being a professional, then, requires that we continue to grow in all of these areas, and this means not only occasional continued education in some traditional sense of the word but also some regular supervision, acute observation and critical feedback on our own pastoral work by another professional. Glasse, in a lecture, put it very sharply: "If we don't know what we're doing, we'll never know whether we've done it or not." To be a professional means to be able to make some determination about whether we are doing our work in an effective manner.

This would seem to require continued supervision of our own work. It is quite possible to learn certain ways of communicating and eliciting communication, then go on in pastoral care, preaching, teaching, etc., convinced that because effective methods have been learned and even at one time practiced, it is therefore inevitable that performance will continue at a high level. This is patently not so, as demonstrated by the experience of persons in many professional groups. It has certainly not been my experience in such major ministerial functions as preaching and pastoral care, including pastoral counseling. I have discovered in myself a tendency to grow lax in such a minutely graduated diminishing way that week by week the lowered level of performance is noticeable neither to me nor some number of people who are listening to the preaching, or who are recipients of the pastoral care. But alert professional critics and supervisors, and occasional alert and concerned lay persons, have from time to time been able to point to the specific behavior which is its own proof of diminished effectiveness, the evidence of misjudgment, and habits which reflect lessened competence.

Regardless of what a minister's approach to an understanding of psychodynamic theory or personality may be, regardless of the particular style of communication, still the essential ingredients of a helping relationship as presented by Carkhuff hold great promise for upgrading pastoral work, preaching (as a later chapter will attempt to show), and even educational and administrative work. It would also seem necessary to seek to establish a structure within which we could discover from other professionals whether these ingredients are regularly a part of our pastoral relationships and conversations at a high level. Specifically, any of us ministers can profit from the regular supervision of our own pastoral practice, to the glory of God, for the benefit of those persons and families in need to whom we are related, and for our own fulfillment as persons and as professionals.

We have seen in the development of the points of this discussion the continual intertwining of person-pastor-professional, at every level of living and functioning. Carkhuff has stressed the point that the right to help can no longer be given just by a person's role but only by the quality of an individual's personhood and his/her ability to communicate this in a relationship with another so that the other is led into significant growth. Carkhuff would choose as a goal the populating of the entire world with persons who can effectively be responsible in helping others.[15] These would be the persons without whom the home, the church, and the community would be a cold place where humanness is lacking and perspectives dictated only by the events of the moment. So many of those moments in our lives at critical times have the power to crush hope, to bring despair, and in which fear and fantasy have free reign. None of us would be so presumptuous as to claim that no doctors, nurses, social workers, teachers, psychologists, lawyers, persons in business or others provide these human elements or share their faith. Certainly some number of them do. But we ministers are the professional persons whose primary responsibility is to furnish these elements in whatever situation or set of relationships we find ourselves, to stimulate others to do so, to hold the show together, and to participate in the creation and re-creation of the meaning of the human drama that is unfolding. It takes a real professional, a high quality of person, a person of faith. This is the type of person whom we seek to *be* within the context of the congregation and its larger community setting as we function as pastors.

II. The Context: Church as the Family of God

We ministers understand ourselves in a variety of ways, and we differ from one another in the amount of emphasis we place on these collections of self-understandings of ourselves. We are ministers *of God.* We are ministers *to His people,* by which we usually mean in practice, to *all* persons, as well as to the "people of God," a formal reference to the church. Yet no matter where we place our emphasis and how we go about doing what we do, we all *are,* in fact, ministers of *the church.* Regardless of how we conceive of and talk about our reasons for going into the ministry, it is the church that ordains us, provides the means of our support (financial and otherwise), gives continuing affirmation and its seal of approval to our ministry, whatever it is, and is the context of our ministry, even though we may work in many locations other than the local parish.

If we are to understand ourselves with greater clarity as persons and professionals, if we are to maintain perspective on the ministerial activities we perform, and therefore be more effective in our functioning, it is important to understand our context, the church. In examining some of the biblical materials related to the community of faith, then applying relevant psychiatric research to a valid concept of the church, we have the possibility of understanding more clearly the practical meaning of our life together. In turn, our task in and for the congregation might be focused in such a way that we gain a new perspective on the complex group life that we have. This should lead to a re-evaluation of the style and goals of our congregational leadership functions.

The Family of God

There are many images offered in the Bible and by other streams of our tradition to assist us in understanding who it is we are as the church: the body of Christ, the new Israel, the fellowship of believers, saints, the people of God.

One image which is not stated explicitly in the Bible and which does not seem to be in common use, but which has its roots in a variety of early Christian statements and which continues to have a clarifying and guiding force for us today, is the image of the church as the *family* of God. As obvious as this term might be once we get it out before us, it is surprising to note not only that it is *not* used in the Bible, but that the Greek word *patria,* family, is used only three times in the entire New Testament (Luke 2:4; Acts 3:25 and Ephesians 3:15). None of these *directly* suggest the term "family of God" as a designation for the church.

The first foundation for supporting the Biblical nature of the family of God as a way of referring to the church is not one merely of accumulating relevant texts, but is to be found in understanding the whole thrust of the Old Testament as defining the identity of the Jewish people as a single cohesive unit in the midst of other groups of people and of the New Testament as defining the church, the *ekklesia* (literally the assembly of the people) in the same way. The Christian life is not "my God and I" but *our life together* as the *people* of God.

There are a number of ways of approaching the development of this theme. Certainly the centrality of family life in the Old Testament is apparent. The first *group* responses to God were those of families, or of the father on behalf of the family. The first tribes were extended families, including the servants, of course, within the family life. A family in some sense was all of those who claimed kinship, not necessarily by blood, with the father. These were the first people of God, with the family origin and group response to God giving the definitive boundaries of the word "people." The people of God were not people in general, people of all nations, but they were a cohesive unit, *like* a family or tribe. It was a definable relation, with a sense of belonging.

Israel was made up of a confederation of these tribes, or extended families. "At that time, says the Lord, I will be the God of all the families of Israel, and they shall be my people" (Jeremiah 31:1). But at the same time the *whole* nations of Judah and Israel were referred to as families, so the large confederation of families was itself definable *as* a family. "Have you not observed what these people are saying, 'The Lord has rejected the two families which he chose'?" (Jeremiah 33:24). Amos made clear the identity of the nation and the family when he said, "Hear this word. . ., O People of Israel, against the whole family which I brought up out of the land of Egypt: 'You only have I known of all the families of the earth' " (Amos 3:1-2a). The development from family to tribe to nation, all the people of God, was through Abraham, who by his faith in God was the original father (Genesis 12:1-3; 15:5-6).

In the New Testament, Christians are also spoken of as Abraham's sons, as Paul is making his point that the true descendants are those who have faith in God, "all those who share the faith of Abraham" (Romans 4:16). "So you see that it is men of faith who are the sons of Abraham" (Galatians 3:7). The church was in effect sharing the inheritance that was God's promise in the original covenant. We are his, Abraham's, God's, continuing family.

Another connection is made which simply emphasizes the same point when we examine the use of the word "house" and "household" in the New Testament. Again, the term was rooted in Old Testament usage.

"Behold, the days are coming, says the Lord, when I will make a new covenant with the house of Israel and the house of Judah . . . I will be their God, and they shall be my people, (Jeremiah 31:31, 33b). Notice the interchangeability between the words "house" and "people." The use of "house of Israel" was continued in the early church's memory of Jesus (Matthew 10:6; 15:24). I Peter refers to the church as "a spiritual house" (2:5), expressed a few verses later as "a chosen race, a royal priesthood, a holy nation, God's own people" (2:9), and, even more explicitly, "the household of God" (4:17). Minear, too, speaks of "this idiomatic identification of household or family with Israel."[1] Pederson, in an analysis of this same issue, stated: "(the family) is the basis of all definitions. . . . It immediately presents itself when the Israelite wants to define a community."[2] It is legitimate, then, to use the term family in this Jewish people-Christian church tradition whenever a social unit bears "the impress of a common character."[3] Finally, Minear declares that the church is a contemporary community clearly identified by "its participation in a common tradition, a history understood as the continuing life of a common ancestor."[4]

The conclusion, definitely, is that speaking of the contemporary church as "the family of God" has its roots in the whole thrust of the central theme of the Bible.

In addition, there are common New Testament terms which naturally stimulate images of the family when we are thinking of the church, especially when heard in the light of the primary point just made concerning the essential concept of the people-household-family in Jewish life, and, consequently, in the life of the early church.

Many times we are referred to as the "sons of God" (Romans 8:14-17, 23, Galatians 4:5, Ephesians 1:5, and others). In Matthew 12:50 Jesus is saying, "For whoever does the will of my father in heaven is my brother, and sister, and mother." Jesus' characteristic word for God was Father, not only the word *pater,* which literally means father, but on occasions the word *abba,* an Aramaic word of intimacy and familiarity, as a child today would say, "Daddy." He taught us to say, "Our Father." And when we choose to say that together, we choose one another as our family in the sense of the mutual agape love (acting for the well-being of one another) and responsibility and sharing which that implies. But even though we respond in this way, the origin and quality of life of this family is grounded initially upon the action of the Father. In Matthew 23:8-9, it states, "You are all brethren . . . for you have one Father who is in heaven." Our role with one another in this family is to "strengthen your brethren" (Luke 22:32). In the early church, the New Testament makes clear through many references (174 times, according to Paul Minear), the term brothers (and we must also say sisters) is a very common way of addressing fellow Christians and a congregation as a whole.

Practical Implications

The church is the family of God. We are the church. What does this mean for us? To think and speak of ourselves as the family of God has a number of practical implications for our actual life together in congregations.

Self-Identity

First, the purpose of the family is that of mutual need-fulfillment, and *one* of the major needs, if not *the* major need, is to provide self-defining experiences for each family member. By this is meant that each person is provided those sorts of experiences which encourage the development of clearcut, but at the same time flexible, ego boundaries, that is, the ablity to know oneself as oneself, separate from others. But in the family we are also provided with experiences which lead to effective and meaningful styles of interacting with one another, with this actually being dependent upon having a clear sense of our own personhood.

So, first, the purpose of the family is to provide self-defining experiences, and therefore the image of the church as the family of God emphasizes the central force of the life of the church as providing self-defining experiences for ourselves in this world: "I am a member of the family of God, a child of God, and it is with this identity that I act out life in the world and in relationship to other persons." A primary issue, however, is how such identity is given and received in families. To understand this process of identity development it is important to view the family not just as a group of individuals, but as a system.

The Church-Family System

Studies of families demonstrate that the family is a system, a single organism in a sense, just as each one of us is a single organism. Paul's analogy of the church as a body, comprised of many members, was a very appropriate one. Each one of us has a variety of individual organs which are linked together. Generally, when we are functioning well, these organs work together for our benefit within our particular system. If one part of our system malfunctions, then the whole organism feels it in some way. When this happens, certain other parts of the organism adjust to make up for it. A fever rises too high, then we have a chill. Usually, the chill, when it comes to an end, is accompanied by heavy sweating, another adjustment process seeking to bring body temperature back to its approximate normal state. This is referred to physiologically as homeostasis, or the homeostatic principle, as the different organs of the whole body are constantly operating to maintain a relatively stable physiochemical balance within the person for that person's health and most effective functioning. Obviously, we must realize that in the extreme, either the body cannot adjust, or the adjustment itself is dangerous.

The same process holds true of families. The concept of family homeostasis is a very important one. Even though families may differ from one another in many ways, every family develops its own internal operations that seek to maintain the family as a unit while trying to meet the needs of the individual members. Unfortunately, some families do this very poorly, and therefore to the detriment of its individual members, and some families accomplish this dual function (maintaining itself as a unit *and* meeting the needs of its members as individuals) quite well.[5] This reality leads us to a third consideration of what it might mean to conceive of the church as the family of God.

The Healthy Family of God

As a family system, the nature of our church life together can be guided for our benefit by the results of an extensive study of the characteristics of healthy families. It has been axiomatic for some years now that different qualities of self-concepts and different levels of happiness and effectiveness in living are dependent upon the nature of the particular system of the family of origin. For example, granting the influential force of early trauma which cannot be controlled, and possible other non-controllable factors, certain sorts of family systems tend to have more schizophrenic patient family members than others, certain other types of families more neurotic members than others, et cetera. Only recently, however, has it become possible to identify in a clear way the characteristics of the healthy family. Our assumption might be—and this is the thesis of this chapter—that congregations are like families in that they operate according to different principles, and, therefore, are different systems. Some of these systems contribute more to the mental health and overall growth of its members while some tend to contribute more to their distress and dysfunction. Certainly, the idea that certain congregations may vary in the quality of their life together, or that there may be disturbing and dysfunctional elements in them, is no surprise. This varying quality of congregational life, the life of the family of God, gave rise to several of Paul's letters and to specific evaluative comments and bits of advice, as well as to a special word from the Lord in a number of instances. And, we cannot avoid noting varying degrees of health in different congregations today.

By using the term mental health to refer to an outcome of congregational life might raise questions in some person's minds. Is mental health the purpose of the church? Certainly, mental health is not identical with the meaning of the term Christian salvation. But neither are they unrelated. Clearly no one would suggest that it is irrelevant to the church (or to God himself) whether the well-being of persons is produced and sustained by participation in congregational life or whether persons are led into unnecessary distress, overdependence upon external authority, rigid repression of emotions, a lack of openness in relationships, and other dysfunctional reactions.

To the contrary, there is a positive relationship and an

overlapping in meaning of Christian salvation and mental health, although they are not the same. The purpose of the life and mission of the church is referred to by various terms in the New Testament, very frequently by the words salvation and reconciliation, although the terms kingdom of God and eternal life and some others are also used. The word salvation comes from the Latin root word meaning health. Other related words of the Germanic languages demonstrate the conceptual overlapping between salvation and health, healing, and wholeness. The ministry of reconciliation to which Paul specifically calls the church in II Corinthians 5 means to function in such a way as to bring persons into committed relationship with God through Christ and with one another in a community of faith. These two words, salvation and reconciliation, are words which complement one another in their emphasis as being the work of the church. To be a Christian means to be a part of the community of faith which is functioning in *this* way. Therefore, salvation (health, wholeness) can never be conceived of as an individual matter alone. To enter the salvation life is to be reconciled with God, with one's own inner being, and with other persons. We are not whole if we are separated from God and from others.

It is important to note that the Jewish idea concerning the wholeness of the person is identical with that of the contemporary psychosomatic approach: it is a dynamic interrelation of our physiological, cognitive, and affective (emotional) processes. Jesus understood the will of God to include the wholeness, the health, or the salvation of the individual person, in relation with others, in a supportive community that receives its identity and strength from its conscious covenant with God.

The healthy family study to which reference has been made and which will form the basis for much of the remainder of this chapter, was made by the Timberlawn

Psychiatric Foundation of Dallas.[6] The study has covered a period of several years, beginning initially with distinguishing between families defined as healthy (that is, no member had found it necessary to undergo psychiatric treatment or had been in trouble with the law) and families in which there was a hospitalized psychiatric patient. A second phase of the study discovered that it was possible within the healthy families themselves, all of which were drawn from a single church congregation, to distinguish between those which were operating at an adequate level and those which seemed to be functioning at an optimal level. This chapter will summarize the characteristics of the optimally functioning healthy family, and examine how each of these characteristics may be applicable to the minister, to congregational life,or to both.

The first major distinction to notice between families is the continuum between entropy and negentropy, terms taken from studies of the physical world. Entropy refers to the degree to which the family is an absolutely closed system, with no openness to energy or input from the outside, and where life structures tend progressively to disintegrate. Negentropy describes a system with structures, but one which is open to energy coming into the system from the outside, so that new energies are always available. The structures are flexible and are continually being revitalized. Families, like any system, may be placed on a continuum from those which are disorganized and chaotic through those which hold together, but do so only by a closed rigidity, on to those which have organized structure, but which are open and flexible. Congregations as families of God may also be observed at all points on this continuum, with the resulting range of negative to positive contributions to the lives of their members.

As the characteristics of the families on the healthy end of the continuum begin to be specified, it is very important to note that even though these characteristics have been identified and can be listed with precision, it does not mean that the families all look alike. Their health in their life together, therefore their continuing mental and emotional health-giving powers to their members, seem to be independent of styles of living in terms of the outward forms we observe: the particular belief systems, the characteristic language patterns, or specific activities. This seems to be important to note as far as congregations are concerned because the conclusions are not going to support any church which might be saying that their particular verbal formulation of Christian faith, their creeds and details of doctrine, their precise form of worship, the particular constellation of activities which mark their congregation, is *the* way.

The first characteristic to be noted is that the optimally functioning families demonstrated an affiliative in contrast with an oppositional attitude.[7] They expressed love and warmth toward other members of the family. It was open and genuine. Out of this love grew a genuine commitment to one another and to the family unit. In addition, "the expectation that encounters were apt to be caring encouraged reaching out to others."[8] Certainly, love and commitment to one another was a part of the uniqueness and power of the early church. The writer of I John expressed this attribute: "We know that we have passed out of death into life because we love the brethren" (3:14). The writer of Ephesians stated, "I have heard of . . . your love toward all the saints" (1:15), and to the Thessalonians Paul wrote, "And indeed you do love all the brethren" (I Thessalonians 4:10).

As a function of that love the members of optimally functioning families had a high degree of respect for the uniqueness of one another in thought, feeling, and act. This is not at all to suggest that there were no behavioral guidelines. There were. But there was great respect for one's own subjective world and those of other family members, a second major characteristic of the healthy family.[9] This means taking seriously and being able to express openly what is meaningful to me and what my feelings are, and also taking seriously those same expressions on the part of others, leading to significant interchange, growing out of both similarities and differences in belief, perspective, and feelings. There were no rigid belief systems to which every person was required to conform in order to be a good member of this family, nor was everyone's experience of a particular event required to be the same. At the same time they were able to have clear-cut, yet flexible guidelines for behavior, including family ritual, behavior related to health and safety, family order, and moral standards.

It is not difficult to think of congregations which are at different points on the continuum in regard to love and warmth and commitment to one another, and the degree to which they not only allow but support their members in what is important and meaningful to those individual persons within the life of a congregation. The community of faith which contributes most to mental health will have these distinguishing marks as the undergirding foundation of its life. Congregations will contain individuals, and whole denominations will contain congregations, with differing styles and emphases: conservative and liberal, different verbal formulations of faith or different meanings behind the same words, who realize that *my* way of experiencing God through Christ and *my* most meaningful and effective forms of expressing that experience through my words and behavior are not necessarily normative or determinative for any other person's experiences and expressions. The New Testament is full of such differences of experiences and ways of talking about them meaningfully. In the early church there were numerous different terms and analogies to seek to express the significance of Jesus and his relationship with God: Lord, Christ, Son of God, Son of Man, Son of David, the Word, and others. There were the different terms to refer to the direction and goal of Christian life: salvation, the kingdom of God, the kingdom of heaven, eternal life, everlasting life, and reconciliation. There were the several different ways of trying to put into words the marvelous mystery of God's saving act in Jesus. There was Paul's illustration of the body with its different parts, and the variety of gifts from the same Spirit. The individuals and congregations of the early church had their many differences, yet they loved one another, they sought to understand one another, they were committed to one another and to their common Father. So also must our life be if we are to be a healthy family of God and contribute to the growth and well-being of one another, the establishment of our identity as his people, with "the mind of Christ."

A third major category which describes the optimally functioning family was the nature of the high quality of relationship between the parents and the way in which they held the balance of power within the family.[10] The relationship of love and respect between the husband and wife, the openness and the clarity of their communication with each other, the degree to which they meet one another's needs, combine to be the best gift that parents can give to their children. If they do this, they not only provide an excellent model of a meaningful relationship for the children, but they each and together are freed to respond to the children's genuine needs. In the healthier families there is not only such a relationship between husband and wife, but this relationship guarantees a firm coalition when dealing with the children. There are no parent-child coalitions against other family members.

Not every aspect of these characteristics of families can be taken over exactly and applied to a congregation, but certain important parts can. For instance, in a congregation which contributes the most to the growth and health of its members, there are clearly defined structures of leadership. There is an ordered, not a chaotic and confused life. There are neither open nor behind-the-scenes manipulators, or, to the extent that some try to operate in this manner, they are not allowed to do so. Those who are designated the leaders *are* leaders, literally those who take the lead. This, of course, does not mean that non-designated leaders may not take the initiative in a variety of appropriate ways, but there are no covert power brokers. The organization in a church is necessarily more complex than that of a family, but we might, for example, conceive of the local parents of the family of God to be the minister, the staff, and the lay leaders, as they work with each other as individuals and through boards and committees, using both spontaneous and structured forms of communication.

Within the leadership itself, while there are natural disagreements and even conflicts, there are no coalitions formed by some of the leaders with certain other members of the congregation against other leaders and other congregation members, making for confused perceptions of who the leaders really are, mixing up channels of communication, and thus leaving many of the designated leaders and most of the congregation feeling confused and helpless and even angry, without knowing how to go about expressing their needs and their anger clearly and constructively.

Yet, although the leadership structures are clearly defined, they are open and flexible, not authoritarian, and there are designated channels of communication to the leadership. The parents of the healthy family of God invite input, seek consultation, and are open not only to information, but also to feelings. Issues are resolved by the process of "respectful negotiation."

A fourth major notation about the optimally functioning families was that there was a rather high energy level on the part of its members, and that this energy was channeled into quite a variety of both inside and outside the home activities.[11] Some of these were oriented directly toward the family together, to individual family members, or to the whole group. Many others, though, were individual pursuits outside the home, and family members often enough had quite dissimilar interests and engaged in different activities. Even these, however, could be seen as indirectly family-related in that they grew out of the life-style of a particular family, contributed to the growth and well-being of the individual, who then brought his or her own lively personality and discussion of interests and activities and new learnings to the others. The family as a whole was having a constant flood of input from the outside world, resulting in growth, and strengthening it as a unit.

This image is clear enough for the family of God. Can you picture the dull, lifeless, uninterested and uninvolved congregation? Of course you can. There are a number, but they really are a contemporary contradiction of the New Testament church. The family of God is energized by the life of the Spirit. Its model is the continuing creative activity of the Father and the redeeming work in the world of the number one Son. What the different members of the congregation do as individuals or small groups is an outgrowth of their own response to the family's overall commitment to one another and to the world and of their own life-styles, not a matter of coercion or the force of someone else's expectation. While there will continue to be central whole-family activites such as worship, and the collection of sub-units for Christian education, the other specific areas of initiative may vary considerably: the various aspects of the business of the local congregation, local housekeeping chores, personal or group evangelism, working with the poor, the sick, those ignored groups and individuals on the periphery of the mainstream of our society, with minority groups, community education, day schools, agencies that meet particular needs (such as mental health, alcoholism, drug abuse) and many others, *all* out of one congregation, *all* members one of another, *each* going out, then coming back in to report, to share, to stimulate, to enlarge perspective, to increase concern, to assist in the growth of the whole family, and no one condemned or put down or left out because "you're not interested in what I'm interested in, or you're not doing what I'm doing." There are also entire congregations which, while containing some variation within their own membership, tend to participate more in one major thrust of the Christian community or of Christian outreach than others. There are congregations with a more traditionally defined evangelistic outreach, others majoring in very sophisticated lay theological education, or yet others in a variety of forms of Christian social action, or one which both goes out to alcoholics and welcomes alcoholics into their midst, and on and on, almost endlessly. But we are *all* children of the same Father. We are the *family* of God, and this is our joy and our richness, our initiative and energy, and our *diversity* of activity.

A fifth characteristic of the healthy family was the quality and quantity of their communication.[12] They talked with each other. They shared information, ideas, and feelings about themselves and one another. They did not expect others to read their minds. ("You should have known that I wanted this or needed that.") They reacted openly and said what they wanted from one another.

Especially notable were four aspects of communication:

First, the verbal expression of emotions in a clear and direct and appropriate manner was understood to be a normal part of living together. No emotion was taboo to feel or talk about, whether it be love, joy, sexual feelings, sadness, anger, or whatever. It was recognized that feelings are only feelings. They are not necessarily good or bad in and of themselves; they are not harmful. They merely *are,* and are a part of us, and it is not only all right but very important to talk about them.

Second, communication in these families was very spontaneous. People blurted out what was on their minds. They interrupted one another, and while a person who was interrupted might claim his/her time to finish, no one was squelched or put down or made to feel that he/she had no legitimate contribution.

Third, the purpose of most communication was to understand rather than to seek agreement, and such understanding was frequently achieved. We *always* need to understand and be understood. We do *not* always need to agree. When we *do* need to agree, and there are occasions, of course, we cannot possibly reach that goal without first going through understanding, so understanding is always the significant purpose of communication.

Finally, they did not often invade one another's personalities either in their verbal or nonverbal behavior.[13] Communication reflected that family members were individual persons, and that they had a right to their own thoughts and feelings. Only rarely in the healthy family did one hear statements like, "Oh, you really don't want to do that." Or, "You don't really mean, or believe that." Or, "You're not really angry at mommy." Or, "My wife and I always think so and so."

By contrast, in far too many of the congregations I have known and heard about there has been an overabundance of guardedness in communication. "If that other person really knew what I feel about this or think about that, or believe about something else, then he wouldn't like me, accept me, think I was a Christian or whatever." There is the fear of being rejected as a person, or not being considered a member of one's *own* family. The additional tragedy is the degree to which we ministers, and often enough our families, too, get caught up in this. So we become guarded, personally closed, defended: in our preaching, in our personal conversations with members of the congregation, in our pastoral care and counseling. "If they knew what I really believed, if they knew how human I really am, the temptations I experience, the weaknesses and contradictions and conflicts I'm aware of in myself." So we attempt to give the image of Superman (or Bionic Woman, the "Six Million Dollar Clergyperson,") and our people are without a living model of openness and clarity of personal communication and self-disclosure. This is unhealthy. It is unhealthy for us ministers and our own families, unhealthy for the members of our congregation, as individuals and families, unhealthy for our corporate congregational life, and it weakens our witness in the larger community.

Now I do not mean *no* restraints, *no* discretion, letting it *all* hang out, becoming verbal exhibitionists. But the healthy family of God will have constant communication between its individuals and within its groups about their activities and perspectives. We will share these with one another, including our feelings about ourselves and one another, and about our honest beliefs. We will recognize and experience that all of our feelings are part of God's creation, and are therefore His gift to us. We will strive more for understanding than for agreement. We will not invade one another's personalities through our language by speaking for one another. We will speak for ourselves, and allow, even encourage, others to do the same. And we will accept one another at all times as members of the family.

A final characteristic of the optimally functioning family as identified by the Timberlawn study is that the members have considerable ability to take responsibility for their own behavior.[14] There is very little scapegoating, or blaming others for one's own behavior.

We are aware of the existence of the "blaming others syndrome" within the family of God, within congregations, between congregations within a denomination, and between some denominations. Even though we may fall into it from time to time ourselves, when we are *most* honest with ourselves, it looks and sounds and feels unhealthy. It is not representative of "the mind of Christ." If we can first seek to *understand* the other, and second, take responsibility for our *own* behavior while allowing the other person to take responsibility for his/her own behavior, and third, work together for our family, then we move in the direction of health.

Families and the Family of God

What has been described here in applying in some rather selective and limited ways the results of a healthy family study to the image of the church as the family of God is really a two-way street. All of us bring to the community of faith ourselves as we are, products of our own families of origin, and, for many of us, participants in a present family which we have chosen to create. We introduce naturally into the congregation the forms of thinking and feeling about ourselves and others, those forms of relating to and communicating with others, that are characteristic of ourselves within these other families. Candidly, this means a number of different levels of emotional and mental and interpersonal health or negatively, maladaption and dysfunction and distress. So the family of God is a mixed bag, because we are in it.

But the family of God also has its characteristic forms of self-identity. We are a family *because* we have been called into being by our Father, through the person and events of Jesus, the Christ, our Brother. We have chosen to respond to this initiative, and therefore have chosen one another in a sense. Our purpose as a family is to continue to act out the "being-for-others" of Jesus Christ, incarnating the love of God for ourselves, for one another, and for the world. We also gather together to celebrate our being as a family within this self-definition. Therefore, there is the impetus to love one another as Christ has loved us. And so the model of our concrete life together, God's being-for-us, if that congregational life has the characteristics of the optimally functioning healthy family, may directly minister to our own personal needs for growth, change, and redemption. It may also stimulate, motivate, and guide our own individual family units in ways which have potential for establishing in us the characteristics of the healthy family, and, therefore, maximizing our own mental and emotional health, or, as Wesley put it, "holiness, happiness, and love."

III. The Word in Proclamation: Meeting Persons' Needs Through Preaching

With few exceptions we ministers like to think of ourselves as effective preachers, and we like to think that others think of us in the same way. Preaching is our regular public appearance, and both our own egos and our genuine desire that people respond positively to the gospel are involved in our not wanting to fall on our faces in the pulpit. For most clergy in the parish, regardless of the functions to which we attach importance during the week, and regardless of the way in which we order our time (what we *say* is most important and how we spend our time are often quite different things), the worship service and its sermon are a climax toward which the week builds. The congregation gathers to remind each other of who it is we are, God's people, and to seek to discover, or once again to be reminded of what his Word is for us as individuals, as a congregation in this community, and as a whole church in his world today.

Of course, we are realistic enough to realize that that is not really the most powerful motivation leading all of those present to this place, and even that we ministers from time to time lose sight of what it is we are planning for and doing with regard to worship and to preaching. But when we are *really* aware, this is what we would like to be about. This is the way we hope the congregation understands itself and what is happening; or, at least, realizes that we are assisting them in moving toward this individual and corporate self-consciousness. So for this reason, as well as for the simple, human, personal reason that none of us likes to be publicly embarrassed, we would prefer that people hear our preaching as "good" rather than "bad". By this, we certainly do not mean that persons always need to respond to every sermon with agreement and a feeling of comfort, but that we not be tagged as doing a shoddy piece of work, incompetent, irrelevant, poorly constructed and presented.

If we are not preaching in such a way that important needs of people are being met, then we are not doing any preaching of the Word at all. It would only be irrelevant mouthing. The gospel, no matter which aspect of it is being explicated, always speaks to some real and legitimate human need. Don't misunderstand. I am not suggesting that preaching should always be dealing with those types of issues which arise in the pastoral care and counseling functions of the minister only to be delivered as the subject matter of sermons to a larger group of people. The sermon certainly should not always be explicitly about personal problems, knotty individual or family decisions, conflicts, or crises. Preaching in such a way as to meet person's needs does not imply that the pulpit is to be the regular weekly source of psychological self-help.

To preach, one must know the gospel (not just know *about* it, but *know* it), and being aware of the needs of particular persons to whom he or she is preaching, seek to bring the two together. Tillich's principle of correlation must always be operational for us in sermon preparation. This principle insists that the questions to which the gospel is directed must be genuine, human (existential) issues and that the church's response must be both true to the gospel and framed in language which is understandable by the people to whom it is addressed.[1]

Cleland refers to this as "bifocal preaching,"[2] a focus upon the accurate proclamation of the Gospel and an accurate reflection of the "contemporary situation" at the same time, and he emphasizes that there is no Word of *God* without *both* foci.[3] So preaching *to be understood,* an obvious requirement, assumes preaching *with understanding.*

This pushes us preachers in the direction of developing a proclamation of the whole gospel (not all of it in every sermon, of course, although most of us have at least occasionally found ourselves trying to do so). We must do this in such a way that it touches the people at the point of their individual, family, and other group needs *and* in such a way that they can recognize the need, hear the gospel in relationship to that need, and be more capable of making a response. But, while "preaching to persons' needs," we must certainly always beware of the trap of developing as our image that of the sanctuary as a large couch and the preacher as a stand-up shrink.

I simply cannot agree with Teikmanis' statement that "dynamic preaching is basically pastoral care in the context of worship."[4] Effective preaching may be *supportive* of pastoral care, or to some extent *grow out of* pastoral care experiences, or parallel it in *some* of its goals, but it blurs important distinctions to say that one *is* the other. Within the functions of ministry it is possible to proliferate such "something is really something" statements, all with an element of truth, until none of us knows what we are talking about. We could just as well be saying that "dynamic preaching is good Christian education, or evangelism," or "good Christian education or Christian social action is effective evangelism," or "worship is a form of Christian education," and so on. All of these areas of ministry grow out of the same motivation, share similar goals, are processes involving people, and seek some form of Christian response, but they are not all "basically" the same thing in another context. Preaching is not pastoral care, just as pastoral care is not preaching, although both are at the heart of our task as Christian ministers.

My only points here are, first, if a person hears a sermon and goes away with the question, "But what does this have to do with me and my needs as a human being, or our common needs as a people?" then the gospel has not been fully, accurately, and clearly proclaimed. Second, the one way in which preaching and pastoral counseling *are* alike is that they are both interpersonal, primarily verbal processes engaged in by the minister with others, and as such there are *some* common goals and necessary relational ingredients if they are to be facilitative.

For effective preaching, then, two things are needed: an experiential-intellectual understanding of the Word and an awareness of and an ability to provide those conditions which are necessary ingredients of all interpersonal helping processes.

When the term "effective preaching" is used, rather than its being accepted by us without thinking, as a catch word that rolls glibly off our tongues to describe some ideal content or form of presentation, it should set off an alarm system in us which leads us to challenge its meaning. This alarm might alert us to the possible superficiality of the use of this term and push us toward a recognition of the resistance to change which resides within both us and our congregations, since effectiveness in preaching, as in pastoral counseling, lies in the outcome, the results—namely, commitment and attitudinal and behavioral change on the part of persons.

For us preachers, a major barrier to the change that would lead in the direction of more effective preaching as defined by outcome lies in our own tendency toward self-delusion. This is the way that it works. Members of our congregation who like us, or who like what or how we preach, or are actually helped by it in some way, very frequently tell us so. Even some of those who do not like our preaching suddenly find themselves confronted by us and they feel called upon to say something and cannot think of anything else to say than, "That was surely a good sermon, Preacher." Many others are silent, leaving us to judge their responses primarily in the light of what positive feedback we do get, along with what we would like to believe about ourselves. If someone comes to church only once and never comes back, or someone who has attended rather regularly stops coming, then we either take no notice of this or we reach the conclusion that it is quite obvious that they are not up to taking the proclamation of the gospel, pure and direct, forcefully and effectively proclaimed, as, of course, we are doing it. In other words, many of us grow quite expert at molding our rationalizations out of genuine positive responses to our helping, our guesses about why our preaching gains such a response, plus our desire to think of ourselves as good preachers, into a comprehensive theory which can put the reasons for those persons who are not being helped by us squarely on their shoulders, and we escape the primary responsibility. Rodney Hunter very perceptively points out our indulgence

> in magical expectations of the functions of ministry—such expectations being magical in a purely unconscious way yet all the more powerful for being so. For instance, there is a common belief among ministers that preaching changes people, or at least that "good preaching" does. Such preaching is said to combine a strong biblical thrust with good illustrative material and personal charisma, and be capable of influencing persons at their deepest levels of meaning and motivation, if not indeed "changing their lives." This conviction, so sacred to preachers, persists despite ample evidence to the contrary.[5]

Hunter also reminds us of the unconscious resistance to self-awareness and change which are a part of the inner dynamics of the persons who make up any church congregation, and how relatively unaffected these persons usually are by attractive, rational, and persuasive presentations of all kinds.[6]

Where does this leave us? Is the only conclusion that preaching, too, is a "vanity of vanities"? Shall we give it up because there is no magic? Or will our own resistances lead us to reject Hunter's description of our human condition, even within the church? None of the above! It seems imperative to accept as fact our human resistances to change and the power of self-delusion. Yet it also seems possible to continue to preach, with our hope renewed by insights derived from increased awareness of the dynamic power of the Word and words, when this Word is proclaimed by means of the words of a preacher who is aware of and who provides in this relational process the facilitative conditions of all helping relationships.

The Dynamic Meaning of the Word

The Word is not merely *the* Book or even a message which the Book tells about, and *a* word is not merely a sound or a particular patterning of ink on a page. The word "word" refers to the self-expression of a person. It is initiative-taking in the communication of oneself. It is the personal act of self-revelation. It is the making exterior of that which is interior to one's own being, whether spoken by God or by a human being. So both theologically and psychologically the spoken word is dynamic, and therefore contains within it the potential power to produce change.

The Word: Psychological

Understanding the origins of speech by the human being and the continuing role of words in our lives can assist us in understanding more fully what is meant theologically by the Word of God, and therefore what it is we are referring to when we speak of preaching the Word. What is the meaning of the word spoken from one person to another?

When we observe carefully, we discover that a word is never *merely* a word. It is, as stated above, a reflection of who we are, an acting out of our being in relation to another being. In order to grasp fully this level of the meaning of spoken words, an elaboration of the development of personality and the role of the learning and use of language in the early development of the child would be necessary. Such a detailed elaboration is obviously beyond the scope of this book, and, in fact, is to be found in an earlier work.[7] Only a very brief summary will be presented here.

Talking is originally learned by every child in the context of the highly emotionally charged relationship of absolute dependence upon the parents. The original meaning of talking then gains its full force from the potency of this relationship in the development of the selfhood of the child. It is learned in a very complex process, combining the beginning natural expression of sounds on the part of the child, the imitation of whatever the parents are seeking to teach by a method of rewarding certain sounds over certain other sounds, and by actual identification with the talking behavior of the parents. This last factor means that the language of the parent and the attitudes which the parent has toward the child are incorporated by the child as a part of his or her own self. Language, then, is literally an integral part of oneself. It is not just what we *do,* but who we *are.* Talking is practiced by the child, first, as a necessary means of communicating basic survival and comfort needs, second, as a means of winning and maintaining parental approval, and third, as a means of holding the parents emotionally near even when the child is alone. In all three of these ways talking is a learned method of overcoming separation. Out of our basic need to maintain ourselves as human beings, we continue to relate in meaningful ways with other persons, and talking is one of the most important ways that we have of doing this. Relationship is a two-way street, the giving and receiving of ourselves to and from one another. The verbal communication of meaning, emotional and intellectual, is a necessary part of this relationship-beginning, developing, and maintaining process. The power of the spoken word, then, is the power of being itself. The word is emotional-relational in its very nature, and it encompasses all the time dimensions—past, present, and future—of our lives. These very meanings of human words in our relationships with one another can be carried over to enhance our understanding of the Word of God when it is spoken to and through us.

The Word: Theological

In a way it is ludicrous to have a brief section which purports to deal with the concept of the Word of God. However, it would be unthinkable not to make the type of comment which would clarify and emphasize the dynamic quality of the Word. Any analysis of the biblical material shows the identification of the *Word* of God and the *act* of God. God speaks, and something is *done.* The Word has the power to create, to produce order within creation, to purify, and to save. God speaks his Word, and things and people change. The Word is always acting, and it manifests itself in a variety of forms. Mary Daly suggests the use of verbs rather than nouns to *name* God,[8] perhaps a strange thought to some today, but hardly radical for a biblically based theology. "I am who I am . . . say this to the people of Israel, 'I am has sent me to you' " (Exodus

3:14), among other possibilities, seeming to mean "I am the one who is *doing* this, who is now *calling* you to *action,* who through you will *set my people free. Do* this, and then you will truly discover *who I am."*

If God is creating and redeeming acting, there is no way in which his Word could ever be accurately conceived as static, or as some*thing* which could be used and manipulated by human beings. For the Hebrews whose life is reflected in the Old Testament to use the word *Word* in reference to God demonstrates that they had experienced God's *acting* in their lives, and that they had experienced the dynamic power of words in their awareness of themselves as human beings and in their relationships with one another through the creating, linking, changing power of words. Therefore, it was descriptive of their understanding of God to speak of the *Word* of God. No understanding of the Word of God could possibly be complete without understanding the psychodynamic origins of the human language which I summarized in the last section, since this human language itself has given rise to symbols (words) which people must necessarily use if they are to communicate their experience of God. So, while all human words are not necessarily the Word of God, God expresses himself in such a way that human words and acts *may* be his Word.

If God is the source and the foundation of truth, then any word of truth is the Word of God. If he is Savior and Reconciler, then any healing, reconciling word is *his* Word. If he is Creator and Sustainer of the human self, then any word which builds up the self, any word spoken by another to me in the process of the continuing formation of my self, and the word spoken to me by another which sustains and nourishes me, is the Word of God. If he is Judge, then any prophetic words, any words calling me to self-examination, and calling me to throw aside my defenses and pretenses, from whatever human source, are also the Word of God. "The concept of the Word of God . . . does not mean any special, supernatural word . . . but true, proper, finally valid word."[9] According to Ebeling, it is possible to speak in this manner because God is not to be thought of as merely a *part* of reality, or some force which is in addition to reality, with God and his creation being totally separate entities, but rather God's creation is the expression of God himself. So when either God or the world is spoken of, the other is involved as a part of the total event of God's communication. The Word of God is a relational event, an event which is a part of an on-going, continually creating relational process. Therefore, ". . . God's Word is (not) a separate class of word alongside the word spoken between men. . . . "[10] The matter of whether the speaker is *merely* another person or is *both* another person and God himself depends upon the stance of faith of the person who hears and responds to the word. The issue is not who the instrumental speaker is, but whom do *you* hear, not what the informational content is, but how you *respond.*

Did God or Nathan speak? "You are the man" (II Samuel 12:7). God did not speak some unembodied, unmediated word. Nathan chose to confront his king, person to person. He spoke a word of truth, heard and accepted by David as the Word of God to him, with the power to produce an awful self-awareness, a feeling of the need to change, a stirring of the motivation to change, and the power to facilitate change. "David said to Nathan, 'I have sinned against the Lord' " (II Samuel 12:13).

"The power of the words as communication is by no means restricted to information and the increase of knowledge. The power of words as an event is that they can touch and change our very life."[11]

They "touch and change" our lives because they

represent the speaker to us, communicate the other as a person to us as persons. In turn, their words invite response. Therefore, a part of the meaning of the original words is shaped by the responses that are made to them. What we discover in what we have just described is the creation or reflection of relationship between persons, the establishment or confirming of communion. This is Hayakawa's point when he said that "before love, friendship, and community can be established among men . . ., there must be a flow of sympathy between one man and another."[12] This flow of sympathy, or communion, is effected through "affective communication."

At the heart of the meaning of the term "Word of God" is the establishment of communion, relationship. Relationships are always dynamic, always changing, having within them always the potential for the growth of the person involved. When God speaks, he acts to establish, sustain, and build communion with us. When we as preachers preach the Word, that is, speak words in a certain way, in a specified context, God speaks his Word to elicit our response in relation to him.

The spoken word is only one form of communication, of course. In fact, in chronological development, it is second to the act, although it then becomes an additional act which is inseparably linked with the act of the total person, and represents the complete act for which it stands. "I love you," is the act of speaking which properly refers to all of the other acts which express love in our relationship. The spoken word must always have its validity, its truth, tested and confirmed by the total activity of the total person. In the same way, when we speak of the Word of God, what we call the spoken or written word must always be tested and validated by its congruence with the total activity of the *person* whom we also call the Word of God, Jesus Christ.

Only those human words which can stand the scrutiny of this Word, which indeed convey him in some sense by means of their human speaking, can appropriately be called the Word of God. If it conveys the truth about us, if it is prophetic, healing, guiding, sustaining, reconciling, or creative of selfhood, then it conveys Jesus Christ, because these words are all responses to his ministry. In addition, the nature of the judgment, the truth, the healing, guiding, sustaining, reconciling, and the transforming of the self must be defined in terms of these responses to his act of self-giving.

Jesus as the Christ, the Word of God, is essential to Christian faith. For by what other standard would we determine both the motivation and results of our human words? Obviously, most of the time our human words do not fulfill these functions, and do not produce these responses. We defend, attack, cover up, deceive, degrade, and lead astray. Thus, we are of necessity driven to the Word of *God.* And wherever our words are pushed in the direction of corresponding with the Word expressed by God in Jesus Christ, they become for us the Word of God, the words of salvation, and our words convey the message of salvation at no other time.

Only the person of faith hears the Word of God. And yet a person receives faith only by hearing the Word of God, a seeming circularity, a paradox. Yet these are paradoxical statements descriptive of human experience. We have all had the experience of someone's listening to us but not really hearing what we are attempting to say, then at some later time, both listening and hearing with understanding. What made the difference? Often enough, it has been the continued speaking of the words in the context of our growing relationship. Words may be mechanically heard, but not consciously, openly responded to in a direct way. At the same time, the very fact that they were heard mechanically was not without its influence. The words actually made an impression, a literal neurological change in the brain. They also were a part of the means of a change in the relationship. Remember, words are not only an expression of reality, they can *change* reality, or produce a *new* reality. A person who listens to words being spoken, even without clear comprehension, or with defensiveness or resistance, is not precisely the same person he/she was before he/she heard them, nor is the relationship between speaker and the listener exactly the same. To hear at any level makes it possible to hear at another level the next time, with greater understanding or less, with less defensiveness or more: parents repetitiously telling the child the same thing over and over again; advertisers with their excited monotony, printing, speaking, singing the same words *ad infinitum;* the preacher's going over the same ground many, many times ("the old, old story"); a Hitler or a Mussolini, shouting their slogans again and again, slogans at first ignored by most, perhaps ridiculed by some, later heard seriously yet with horror, but finally, at some level believed and responded to.

So with the Word of God. It is spoken, but we do not hear it. But we are not the same, either. It is spoken again. We do not respond. It is spoken again. And it may finally strike a responsive chord, being the repeated stimulus which has played its role in producing a person who is now capable both of hearing and responding.

> When God speaks, the whole of reality as it concerns us enters language anew. God's Word does not bring God into language in isolation. It is not a light which shines upon God, but a light which shines from him, illuminating the sphere of our existence . . . So the event of the Word of God is necessarily bound up with the entire life of language. For if the Word of God brings the whole of our

reality into language anew, then the reality which is already in language is necessarily addressed anew.[13]

Preaching as an Interpersonal Process

Preaching is the self-conscious attempt on the part of a person to speak those human words which are, using Ebeling's term, "true, . . . finally valid," and which also point to Jesus as the Word of God as just discussed, usually in the context of some series of other acts through which we declare and remind ourselves that we are God's people, and must *act* as such. The sermon is comprised of words used by one human being to other human beings. It is therefore a relational process in which the final meaning of what is spoken is clarified and confirmed both by its congruity with Jesus as the Word of God and by the people's response. The transmission process is not a mechanical one, since a word spoken, as I have already tried to clarify, is never merely a word, but the communication of the inner being of a person in relationship with another person. So in relationship, person-to-person, we seek relationship with the One who makes our personhood meaningful.

This is hardly a new idea. Phillips Brooks in the last century said, "Preaching is the communication of truth by man to men," and "Preaching is the bringing of truth through personality."[14] Who the preacher is as a person, what personal relationship he or she already has with some of the congregation, and what quality of relationship he or she is able to establish with the congregation at this point in time, in *this* act of preaching, are not irrelevant to the proclamation of the Word of God. In fact, we do not so much "preach the Word" (as our common expression states it) as we preach in such a way as to reduce the barriers to comprehending, responsive listening to the Word God speaks *through* our words. Preaching is a time when, in the midst of our speaking words and listening to words, God may also speak and act. We do not determine *whether* God will speak or not. We can neither force his Word out into the open with our scholarship, cleverness, passion, or volume, nor can we silence him through our lack of preparation, dullness, confusion, or complexity. But we can *facilitate,* fail to facilitate, or even actually *impede* the openness of persons to that Word when it is spoken. We can prepare the soil for recognition, for receptivity, for responsiveness, or we can contribute to persons' closedness, defensiveness, resistance. We can, both in verbal content and modes of expression, communicate more in one direction or another on the continuum of reality versus unreality, honesty versus dishonesty concerning our human situation and the authentic word of grace as declared in the acts of Jesus as the Word.

So, preaching is always two-dimensional: the time of the act of God, and also the time of the relational process between preacher and congregation. And while these are not identical, neither can they be separated.

Similarities Between Counseling and Preaching

In order to make clear that the application of insights derived from psychotherapeutic research and clinical practice to preaching is methodologically legitimate, it might be useful to examine similarities between the two functions as processes. Counseling may be defined as a process of growth which takes place in the context of a personal relationship in which one person is understood by the participants as being the helper, with the helper responding primarily verbally in particular ways which are especially facilitative to growth.

Being a process, counseling clearly has certain stages. These must be gone through in a relatively chronological sequence. One cannot leap from an early stage to the last stage and expect the most constructive outcome. Nor can one merely stay in the early stages and expect the process to be a successful one. In a somewhat oversimplified manner, one way of looking at the major stages of the process in a linear fashion would be the following: Self-exploration ⟶ the setting of goals ⟶ evaluation of behavioral alternatives ⟶ decision-making ⟶ action.

Actually, the process is not linear at all, but is much more like a circle with continual feedback and reprocessing:

In fact, the process stated in this way is not new to preaching. Without the last stages of decision-making and action on the part of the hearers of the Word, there has been no sermon. The fact that we may emphasize the proclamation as being the time of the action of not only preacher and congregation but also of the Word himself does not change the basic statement. Some meaning must be conveyed in the most facilitative way by the preacher and there must be some response by the people: decision and action. This is what growth means: not just insight, nor feeling better, although these are not valueless, but ultimately decision-making and acting.

However, most people do not reach that point without a period of self-exploration out of which they become capable of setting their own goals. This is of crucial importance. The counselor does not *explore* or probe the person nor does he or she set the goals for the other. The counselor seeks to enable another person to explore him- or herself. Competent goal-setting and decision-making cannot take place without this. Indeed, there is often little inclination to make new decisions without bringing the process through its stages to this point. There is usually the need to remove emotional barriers, lower defenses, reduce conflicts, and build trust in oneself and the other prior to goal-setting and decision-making.

Since we desire something of the same outcome for a sermon that we do for counseling in terms of its human responsiveness, it would seem logical to presume that considerable attention should be given in the sermon to the process of self-exploration that stimulates, enlightens, and enables responsible goal-setting and decision-making for action, and that to push too soon for decision is counterproductive. Likewise, to preach in the area of human needs in such a way that the process does not *proceed,* but simply stays with self-exploration without leading through goal-setting to the evaluation of alternatives and making of decisions, guarantees that whatever is said will never become a sermon.

Second, counseling is not an impersonal process; it is interpersonal, with the growth of persons being the hoped-for outcome.

Preaching and counseling as interpersonal processes are also similar in that there are within persons who need to grow, even at some level *want* to grow, both conscious and unconscious resistance to the very changes which are necessary. The effective counselor must not only be aware of such resistances and be able to recognize them, but he/she must be prepared to respond verbally to the other person in such a way that these resistances may be brought to light, understood, and diminished, allowing the desired goals of the counseling to be obtained. It is the same with the effective preacher.

> Thus, preachers and their congregations can perpetuate one another's illusions that change is possible or that they are changing when in fact the whole dynamic is masking their mutual frustration and despair over their caughtness in resistances that inwardly defeat each other, themselves, and the work of the church.[15]

Such a declaration emphasizes the imperative upon the preacher to take this reality into consideration in sermon preparation and presentation, with the awareness that the conditions under which resistances may be reduced are provided in the dynamic quality of the relationship between persons—in this instance, minister and congregation. What, then, is the nature of the relationship which facilitates openness to self-exploration and change? Can the conditions be specified with precision? How can these be effectively introduced into the already developed structures of preaching and worship? How can we select those words and communicate from the pulpit those attitudes which make possible a development in the quality of the preacher-congregation relationship that increases the probability of people's responding to the Source and Sustainer of our existence, recognizing that as we do so our sermon comes closer to being a vehicle of the Word of God to *these* people at *this* time?

The Presence of God in the Preaching Relationship

If we are to affirm at all the expression of some reality in Buber's statement concerning our meeting the eternal Thou in the authentic I-thou relationships of persons, then this, too, reemphasizes that the quality of relationships which exists between the minister and the congregation during preaching makes a difference in the effectiveness of the proclamation of the Word. Buber contrasts two forms of interaction between persons. One he refers to as an I-it connection, the utilitarian, instrumental use of another person as if that person were a thing, an "it"—using the other, or treating the other as if the other did not have intrinsic value of his or her own, with freedom and ability to think, decide, relate, and act.[16] Some preaching seems to communicate this attitude toward the congregation as the preacher seeks to squeeze, force, or trick people into certain responses, for whatever possible worthwhile goals, as the presentation pleads, cajoles, threatens, or even in sophisticated and subtle ways misleads or bribes. Not only do we devalue the personhood of the other in this type of preaching, but we devalue ourselves, and the God who is not only the original Creator of human life but the continuing Creator with each one of us of our own genuine humanity is not most effectively met within this process, because we are pushing Him away through this depersonalizing process.

The other form of relationship which Buber describes is I-thou, in which the other person is valued as a person, permitting the depths of genuine humanity within each of us to be shared.[17] In such an instance, the eternal Thou, the God who made such a meeting of persons possible, is himself also met.[18] It makes a difference in preaching when, by one's attitude in the pulpit and by the words and presentational forms selected to explain the scripture and to point to its relevance for *us* in *our* place in *our* day, the preacher makes authentic human contact with persons in the congregation.

On a human level, from psychotherapeutic research and clinical practice, also a specialized form of a verbal relational process, certain essential ingredients of the helping relationship have been identified and defined. These conditions cannot "make" or "force" another person to grow, but they are *necessary* for growth to take place. These conditions as described by Carkhuff[19] clarify the nature of the I-thou relationship referred to by Buber, and they are applicable not only to the minister's pastoral care and counseling work[20] but also are quite suggestive concerning other acts of Christian ministry with people, including preaching.

Summary

Preaching is an interpersonal process, not merely an act done by one person *in the presence of* and *to* a group. The words which are spoken by the preacher are in their human sense (psychologically) dynamic; they are expressions of the preacher as a person, and, in one way or another, are responded to by other persons. Christian faith declares that in these human acts, God is also speaking his Word, and it, too, is dynamic, a self-expression. The psychological and theological are combined in the event of preaching.

As an interpersonal process, preaching shares some goals and characteristics with other interpersonal processes, among them pastoral care and counseling. Therefore, it might be enlightening to preaching to examine what may be referred to as the facilitative conditions of any helping relationship. It is to this task that we now turn.

IV. The Word in Proclamation: The Ingredients of Helpful Preaching

Since preaching is an interpersonal process, this chapter will explore the possibility of adapting to this central event in the life of the church what has been shown to be certain essential ingredients of another interpersonal process, psychotherapy. An elaboration of these facilitative conditions is properly based upon a series of propositions which have a considerable amount of research data to support them.[1]

1. People undergoing counseling or who are seeking help by a process which is primarily verbal do not stand still. They are never merely "not helped." They either get better or they get worse.
2. They get better or worse depending upon whether certain essential ingredients of any helping relationship are present in sufficient quantity and quality.
3. The provision of these identified facilitative conditions for growth is the responsibility of the helping person.
4. It is possible within the psychotherapeutic process to read or listen to any helping verbal response and to make a reasonably accurate evaluation of the quality of the statement in terms of its helpfulness as defined by one or several of these conditions.
5. It is possible for most people to learn to increase the number and quality of their helpful responses.
6. Absolutely basic to the entire process is that the helper needs to *be* a certain quality of person rather than someone who has merely *learned* certain techniques.

The essential ingredients of a helping relationship have been referred to in a variety of forms by many psychotherapeutic clinicians and researchers for many years now. However, when we review the historical sequence which led directly to the ones listed and elaborated by Carkhuff, we see their origin in the work of Roger, in the triad of empathic understanding, unconditional positive regard, and congruence.[2] Carkhuff lists six conditions, which in ongoing research are continuing to be refined, with further ones perhaps yet to be identified. These ingredients, as stated in the propositions above, are not primarily "techniques" which can be learned and used, but are conditions which are truly reflective of the quality of the personhood of the helping person and his or her forms of relating to others. However, since it is also necessary for the helping person to *communicate* this quality of being, the ingredients are not unrelated to forms of verbal and to some extent nonverbal acts. In the discussion of the application of these conditions to preaching, the focus is always to be upon the issue not of how preaching may really become more like pastoral care or counseling, but, utilizing therapeutic insights, how it may become more effective *preaching*—a more powerful proclamation of the Word of God, or, a higher quality of that unique relational process between preacher and congregation, in the midst of which God may act with clarity and decisiveness in our lives.

As these conditions are listed and defined, many ministers will internally say, "Of course. That is self-evident. I already do this." The main purpose in presenting them here is not because the conditions themselves are new, nor because no preacher is aware of them, nor has provided them in his or her relationships (including preaching), but merely to put them all together with sharp focus so as to maintain a constant awareness of their crucial importance, and to push us to think consciously in our sermon preparation week after week of how we may furnish these conditions at a high level of frequency and quality in our preaching.

The Facilitative Conditions Applied to Preaching

The Accurate Communication of Empathy

The first essential ingredient of a helping relationship, absolutely foundational and necessary from the beginning of that relationship, and supporting the entire process throughout, is the accurate communication of empathy.[3] Without it there can hardly be other conditions, and to the extent that the others are present, in the absence of empathy they are relatively useless. As helping persons, we must be able to perceive, sense, feel, and understand where the other person is right at this moment, what that person's present experience actually is, and then in words communicate to the person that we have understood the intellectual content of what he or she has said, that we are aware of the specific feeling or feelings which accompany this particular message, and that we are also aware of the intensity of the feelings. The purpose of the accurate reflection of empathy is to lead a person into that very potent, tremendous, and freeing experience of being understood, helping that person take further steps in self-exploration, which is the major characteristic of the early part of the therapeutic process. If we have the capacity to be where the other person really is at this moment, and we have the ability to communicate this being with and for the other, then the person will feel freer to take another step within the process of self-exploration.

This element of the accurate communication of empathy has always been present in effective preaching, in understanding the persons who make up the congregation, and choosing our words and forms of presentation in such a way that they understand that we understand. The communication of understanding is not merely a prior and necessary condition for the proclamation of the Word, it is itself part of the Word, one source of its dynamic power to facilitate change. The congregation is more capable of experiencing the powerful truth that God truly understands (the One "to whom all hearts are open, all desires known, and from whom no secrets are hid") when they are in the process of experiencing the understanding of the person who at this moment is seeking to preach God's Word.

Jackson is precisely on target when he says:

> The capacity for sensitivity, the ability to feel with and for his people, is a pastor's supreme art. . . . The preacher who is able to move into the thought and feeling of his people . . . creates the mood for effective interchange. In any relationship where there is no chance to talk back, a special atmosphere must be created wherein persons can *feel* back.[4]

Fosdick, in his classic 1928 article on preaching, an article which has yet to be fully heeded, moves head-on into the issue of how to build into the sermon the feeling and thinking responses of people of the congregation in such a way that they feel understood as the people they actually are—at this moment. The preacher may then respond to them, as their situation has just been accurately reflected. Fosdick gives the illustration of a planned dialogical sermon, in which a professor who was a member of the congregation walks up to the pulpit from his pew and begins to disagree with the preacher, who responds, and they proceed to thrash out their differences as a form of the sermon presentation. Then Fosdick goes on to say:

> Any preacher without introducing another personality outwardly in the pulpit can utilize the principle involved in

> this method. If he is to handle helpfully real problems in his congregation, he must utilize it. He must seek clearly and state fairly what people other than himself are thinking on the matter at hand. He may often make this so explicit as to begin paragraphs with such phrases as, "But some of you will say," or "Let us consider a few questions that inevitably arise," or "Face frankly with me the opposing view," or "Some of you have had experiences that seem to contradict what we are saying."[5]

This procedure, which some preachers already use very naturally and others plan carefully, proposes that we introduce verbally into our sermons the present feelings and thoughts, the questions, the doubts, the varying points of view, and the probable challenges of the members of the congregation, verbally representing them to themselves, and then, as a person seeking to represent accurately the gospel, make our verbal responses. When the people feel most understood, then they are at the point of greatest openness to understanding the other, which means understanding the preacher and the gospel to which the preacher now explicitly refers. The methodology, as Fosdick suggests, is to put within the one sermon by one person the best of what "dialogical preaching" has sought to do: demonstrating the preacher-congregation relationship concretely, representing the congregation, representing the gospel *to* the congregation, and responding to the gospel.

The verbal forms with which this internal dialogue may be expressed are almost endless. The more obvious ones, in addition to those mentioned by Fosdick himself, would be something like these:

"A lot (or most, or some) of you may feel . . . "
"Some of you undoubtedly think . . . "
"From what many of you have said to me . . . you believe (or don't believe). . . . "

"Now this may sound like a strong (or foolish, or peculiar) thing to say, but . . . "

"I know that some of you are very angry (or frustrated, or sad) about . . . "

"But some of you may respond, what (why, how) . . . "

Of course, there are numerous less explicit ways to introduce into the sermon words that clearly state an understanding of the persons present.

Naturally, this procedure for the communication of empathy does not assist self-exploration unless there is the accurate understanding of the people in the first place. In fact, the *inaccurate* communication of empathy is destructive to a facilitative relationship, and leads to the experience of *not* being understood, erecting or reinforcing barriers to self-exploration. Both this necessity to understand, and some specific ways of making contact with people for a "listening ministry," is emphasized by Edwards, in a book dealing with *The Living and Active Word,* by calling an essential chapter "How to Hear What Your Congregation Is Saying About Itself."[6]

The preacher must beware of the particular style of presumed "preaching to meet people's needs" which picks up on a particular problem area, labels it, and then gives some "Christian" answers to it. When such an approach slides over into an easy, palliative, "inspirational" sermon, it often does not communicate to persons the depth and complexity and conflicting nature of human emotions and experiences which comprise the reality of their lives, and even though some may "like" the sermon, it does not lead them into the experience of being understood, and thereby not into the difficult process of self-exploration which is the prior and essential condition for effective decision-making and change. To the contrary, such a "clear answer" sermon may add to the stimulation of "good" feelings that only serve to cover up the troubling emotions and the real issues, and, in the midst of such an experience, people continue to lack the facilitating potency of being understood.

Even though counseling does not ignore the rational, and is certainly not anti-rational, and though it must inevitably proceed from some framework of verbal meaning, it still focuses on the feelings of the person from the very beginning and, to some extent, throughout the entire process. Preaching must do the same in order to meet people's needs. People can be assisted to identify, accept, and express their feelings in appropriate ways if the preacher makes clear that he or she (and therefore God, by the way) is aware that they have these feelings, that they are important but that they are *only* feelings, that these emotions are gifts of God, and are therefore basically useful in human life. Then people's needs can be met more fully, conflicts resolved, self-esteem raised, and defensiveness lowered.

The effective preacher must take every opportunity to know the people of a congregation, not only in general, but also in specific detail. The fact that some people, or many people, share similar situations does not necessarily mean that their feelings are identical, or that they have them with the same intensity, or in the same combination. It is the preacher's responsibility to find the words which convey such understanding of the varieties of reactions that people may have to apparently the same or similar situations.

In order to gain such an understanding, the minister must, of course, know himself or herself with some clarity, then take every opportunity to listen to what people are saying about themselves, their relationships, their family life, their work, their needs, and then to explore these in personal and small group conversation in order to gain a confirmed accuracy of understanding. This might even become the material for the verbal communication of empathy in the sermon itself. Finally, it is important for the minister to develop structures for checking the accuracy of his or her communication of empathy in preaching by informal and honest conversation with people in the congregation, and perhaps by organizing sermon preparation and sermon feedback sessions with groups of lay persons.

The accurate communication of empathy is the first essential ingredient which the minister is responsible for furnishing in the relational process of preaching. Far more handicapping to the achievement of our desired goal in preaching (the positive response of people to the gospel, resulting in commitment and growth in Christian faith) than people's going away thinking or saying, "That was a poorly delivered sermon," or "I think the minister missed the point of that particular verse of scripture," or "I think he (or she) was inaccurate with that data," is for people to leave the worship service with the awful feeling, "That preacher just does not understand me at all."

The accurate communication of empathy is the vehicle for the congregation's developing experience of being understood, which in turn makes possible the worshipers' moving into an ever-deepening process of self-exploration, a necessary precondition for increasing insight and attitudinal and behavioral change.

Respect

The second facilitative condition is respect.[7] Respect at the beginning of a counseling relationship means a sense of the other person's worth as a human being and his or her potential for growth, which includes some confidence in that person's ability eventually to make his or her own decisions in a responsible manner. Later in the relationship the respect may grow into a deep personal caring about the other, and we may begin to respond to specific characteristics of the other which are worthy of our respect. It is very obvious that this basic attitude toward another is not communicated primarily (and certainly not exclusively) by the specific words, "I respect you; I value your worth as a person." Rather, in counseling, respect is communicated through our commitment to work with him or her in the helping process, and by our persistent focused attention which enables us to communicate empathy with accuracy. Struggling to understand and coming to understand another person, and sharing that understanding with him or her, is a powerful statement about our sense of his or her worth.

There are, however, a number of ways in which a preacher may convey a *lack* of respect. We may soar over the heads of the congregation, propelled by our fluent use of multisyllabic and esoteric words (like "multisyllabic" and "esoteric"), motivated by our need to impress them with our learning. We may, of course, achieve this particular goal, but in so doing we fail to express our respect for them through the absence of any genuine desire to understand them or be understood by them.

A lack of respect is also conveyed by the opposite approach, when we are patronizing in our tone. Closely related to being patronizing is an authoritarian stance on the part of the preacher, whether subtle and kindly or quite blatant, treating people as if they do not have the capacity to understand, or the freedom and maturity to make their own judgments and decisions. In this style of preaching there is a reflection of a rigid belief system, a failure to present alternative ways of conceptualizing and expressing certain experiences theologically. It is the treating of all issues as if they were black or white and that we, the preachers, always know which is which. There is the failure to consider and put into the sermon the words which suggest the complexity and ambiguity of human feelings and motivations, contemporary social and political situations, interpersonal relationships, and thus the lack of reality which either reinforces some people's narrowly simplistic modes of thinking or leaves them with a sense of the irrelevance of the sermon for their lives, which they experience as quite complex. Respect, on the other hand, is conveyed when the preacher takes seriously the worth and dignity of persons, their ability to think things through, their freedom to make responsible choices for their own lives, although they may do it with our assistance as we suggest appropriate new ideas and interpretations from our undertanding of Christian perspectives and guidelines.

Another way in which the preacher shows a lack of respect is through the "use" of the sermon, or certain parts of it, to manipulate a congregation into making a certain response which the preacher has decided for them, the deliberate attempt to "make" people feel guilty where guilt is not that appropriate, deliberately stimulating emotions for effect only or in the attempt to produce quick and unthoughtful decisions. A lack of respect is also communicated by the slippery use of presumed factual material (whether from the Bible or from the contemporary social scene and contemporary fields of learning), or a subtle bypassing of the steps of logic while maintaining the appearance of logic in moving to a conclusion. Respect is communicated by a rigorous honesty in the use of Biblical materials, by clarifying the steps of the exegetical process rather than merely announcing our conclusions—as if these conclusions were given to us by God apart from the necessary interpretive procedures—also, by rigorous honesty and the way in which factual material from whatever field is handled, and by a consistent logical movement from premise, through illustration and elaboration, to conclusion in the sermon as a whole.

A clue to the nature of a preaching relationship that has a greater probability of leading the congregation into the experience of being respected is furnished by what W. Robert Beavers, a psychiatrist, calls "egalitarian psychotherapy." In the relational process referred to by this term, the therapist invites the client to become a partner in the problem-solving which they mutually agree to undertake. The therapist does everything possible to create an atmosphere of equal power, openness and mutual confidence in order that the process may be satisfying and successful to both parties.[8] Interestingly, Beavers carries this emphasis over into church life when he suggests the importance to some people of being a part of a congregation "that relates to its parishioners as adults" and the value to people of ministers who "go beyond treating adults as children and developing religious thought that is based on the shared search for meaning."[9]

The authoritarian approach is characterized by the language of final conclusions without a visible process, language which discourages questioning and searching, language which does not communicate that the listener has a real part in the process and that without the "right" conclusion on the part of the hearer ("right" meaning the acceptance of the preacher's conclusion) no genuine relationship between preacher and hearer is possible. A preacher friend of mine has described this sort of person by saying of a colleague, "He may be in error, but he is never in doubt." On the other hand, repect tends to be more clearly communicated by language which may be termed tentative or suggestive, inviting the listener to be a part of the searching, struggling, decision-making process.

Tentative language is not wishy-washy language. It does not reflect an "it doesn't matter" attitude, or lack of courage or an inability to take a stand. It simply takes seriously the reality that the minister does not know everything with certainty. Therefore, tentative language reflects accurately those situations which are characterized by complexity, ambiguity, or the possibility of more than one way of viewing them. Tentative language sounds like:

"After serious study, my conclusion is . . ."
"It seems to me as if this is a valid way of viewing this issue."
"One way of saying this is . . . "
"There are arguments on both sides, but as of today my position is. . . . "
"I wonder if a way of going at this is not to . . . "
"It makes sense to me to phrase the meaning of Christ in this way: . . ."

In "egalitarian preaching" there is much stating of one's own thought and the detailing of one's own decision-making processes, one's own views, one's own conclusions and standards, and the most meaningful language for one's own self in sharing Christian experience. These words are affirmative, declarative, inviting, suggesting, even offering, but not demanding or authoritarian, with no attempt on the preacher's part to invade the mind of the other and presume either to force conclusions into the other's head or to act for the other.

This does not mean, of course, that there is no room for the "Thus saith the Lord" statement, the Nathan to David "Thou art the man" confrontation. Rather it means that once the preacher's clearly communicated and demonstrated respect for persons in the congregation has made its impact, such declarative statements have even greater strength because of the quality of preacher-congregation relationship that has been established.

As in "egalitarian psychotherapy," the provision of respect as a necessary condition for the facilitation of growth in faith, and of attitudinal and behavioral change through the relational process of preaching, is accomplished by inviting the congregation to become colleagues in the process of growth in Christian life and commitment. We who are ordained ministers not only may, but certainly should have more technical biblical, historical, and theological knowledge than most, if not all, of our congregation, but this neither means that we know *everything* in these fields nor that we are actually better Christians nor more mature adults nor have an inside track to God. In *fact,* we and our congregations *are* colleagues in the process of the Christian life, with us ministers merely having a professional leadership function. To the extent that we genuinely understand and communicate this reality of our relationship in our preaching to the community of faith, we also communicate our respect for the persons in the congregation. This communicated respect is a necessary ingredient for their fuller response to the Word of God. Hopefully, both the term "egalitarian preaching" and "egalitarian psychotherapy" will come more and more to be accurately descriptive of these interpersonal processes in the future.

Concreteness

The third facilitative condition is concreteness.[10] Most simply this word means what it says, but as an example of concreteness itself, it is necessary to go further and define it more fully. We as human beings do not have problems or feelings *in general.* We have them *in concrete.* Our task in counseling is to assist the other person in being very specific and detailed about feelings and experiences and their meanings, not allowing the other to speak in general or to feel in general. For example, a person may say, "I have really been upset lately." Now this sounds very much like an expression of an emotion, and so it is. But what emotion? How are we to communicate to that person that we understand? We need to know whether the person is upset sad, upset mad, or upset fearful. Therefore we might appropriately respond to the person's statement by saying, "You certainly sound as if something is very distressing to you, but I wonder what you mean by the word upset? How are *you* experiencing it? Precisely what feelings are you referring to?"

In the counseling relationship it is our responsibility to be sure that the other person speaks in concrete terms, gives details, and illustrates. It is also our responsibility to communicate in the same way ourselves, not using mystifying terms and phrases or theological or psychological jargon. Everyday language is the best language, and this is judged to some extent in terms of where we perceive the other person to be.

Concreteness, as every effective preacher has always realized, is essential for clear, accurate, and powerful communication. Fosdick's succinct comment was, "I often think that we modern preachers talk about psychology a great deal more than our predecessors did but use it a lot less."[11] He was referring to that which many of us have both heard and done ourselves, using the language of our new learning in psychology, as well as in other fields, in our sermons rather than expressing in relevant ways the *results* of our new learning in the *usual* language of the people to whom we are preaching. Ferguson may have put his finger on the sore spot for a number of us when he wrote:

> The use of abstract terms in preaching, unless they are specified in terms of the particulars concerned by them, is not communication, but "metacommunication." It is the language we use when we do not know precisely what it is we are talking about.[12]

Ferguson, of course, furnishes for me an example of exactly the point he is trying to clarify when he uses a word like "metacommunication," which leads me to the conclusion that I do not know what he is talking about at that point.

Certainly it is possible for all of us at times to know with some precision the material we are dealing with, but in order to meet our own ego needs we would rather try to impress persons rather than lead them into that essential early stage of preaching, the sense of understanding and being understood. The result is that we impress them only with the idea that we are trying to impress them. Kemp refers disapprovingly to Richard Baxter's practice of preaching one sermon each year that was well above the heads of his congregation just to demonstrate to them what he could do every Sunday if he wanted to.[13] This procedure may do something positive for the ego of the preacher, but it does absolutely nothing for the proclamation of the gospel.

While most of us would agree that in order to facilitate understanding we should avoid the use of technical language, it is important for us ministers to remember that much of our everyday language is, for a large number of lay persons, technical jargon: grace, sin, justification, salvation.

A young woman was talking with me about her "being saved," and went on to say that she did not hear me preaching about it. My response, itself an illustration of concreteness (that is, pushing for clarification and consensus of meaning), was simply "What do you mean by 'being saved'?" There was a long pause. Then very honestly she replied "You know, I don't know. This is just the way I've been talking." Now, by setting aside the language she had learned but which meant nothing to her, for the first time the door was open to our discussing her genuine faith needs and how these might be better met both as a result of this present personal conversation *and* through my preaching.

Concreteness, with its meaning of simplicity, definition, detail, example, and illustration, is a necessary ingredient for preaching that genuinely meets people's needs, preaching that makes it most possible for them to understand God's Word when he speaks.

Genuineness

The fourth essential ingredient of a helping relationship is genuineness.[14] Genuineness refers to the degree to which we are in touch with our own feelings at any given time, our motivations for doing what we are doing. It is the extent to which there is a correspondence or congruence between our own experience and our awareness of the experience. To the extent that important aspects of our own being may be hidden from us by our own defenses and distortions, we will distort the communication of other persons by means of our own needs, and our responses to *them* will also be distorted. It therefore becomes obvious that the process will not result in clarification and resolution of issues for the person needing help. If, for example, we have strong anxiety about death, or sexual feelings, or divorce, or if we have learned how not to feel our anger, then it is very difficult to keep our own feelings (or our defenses against these feelings) out of the relationship when we are visiting a dying person, or someone in grief, or when someone introduces a problem with us that involves strong sexual feelings, or when someone is extremely angry in our presence or does something which stimulates anger in us. These feelings and defenses of ours limit and distort our responses to the other person. Genuineness implies being freely and deeply ourselves in responding to experiences of all types, with an ability to recognize those feelings of ours which may distort or even disrupt the relationship. Once we have recognized and admitted them, then we may either keep these out of the relationship by choice, or, on some occasions, introduce these into the relationship openly in a way that facilitates deeper exploration.

In preaching, as in counseling and in all relationships, we always communicate in some form what our internal reality is. Therefore, when we seek to cover up our own genuine humanity, even to ourselves, we then communicate to the congregation closedness, defensiveness, and lack of self-knowledge. We communicate anger, depression, fear, and sexual conflicts in disguised forms, which are recognized by some members of the congregation, and not so clearly recognized by others. Yet our disguises and distortions of human reality are experienced by them as confusing forces which contribute negatively to their own lives. This inevitable response by persons in the congregation is a barrier to their receiving God's spoken Word to them, since God's Word always begins with a clarification of the truth about ourselves and our need. The preacher's genuineness is a precondition for the clear and undisguised proclamation of the truth about the human condition, which is the necessary first phase of the proclamation of the Word of God.

Self-disclosure

The fifth essential ingredient of the helping relationship is self-disclosure, or one's willingness to allow himself or herself to be known as a human being to the other person.[15] Not only are we *aware* of who we are, including the feelings and motivations that we have at a particular time, but we have the ability to communicate ourselves in appropriate ways to the other person. As is the case with several of the other facilitative conditions, in counseling the matter of timing is very important. Too much self-disclosure too soon can hinder rather than facilitate the other person's exploration. Self-disclosure which is not linked in some helpful way to the other person's needs right at this moment can interfere with the development of both the relationship and the counseling process. However, there does come a point as the therapeutic relationship moves along when it is very appropriate to say something like, "Yes, I've had a similar experience myself," or, "You're expressing feelings which sound very similar to some that I have had. For me it had the impact of . . . , and I wonder if this is what you are trying to communicate." The criteria which must guide self-disclosure for it to be most effective for the other person lie in our awareness of the individual's needs, and of how our self-disclosure might facilitate self-exploration, evaluation of alternatives, or decision-making. We must guard against the kind of disclosure that comes primarily out of the strength of our own need to disclose ourselves. To allow ourselves to become psychological exhibitionists would be destructive not only to ourselves but to the other person as well.

Appropriate self-disclosure gives the other person a point of identification, a sense of being fully understood, and the feeling of being a part of an authentic human relationship. The other person thus becomes a colleague in the human growth process, because permission to admit the truth about oneself provides an impetus to share more of oneself with this person who has now given something of himself or herself within the process.

There are possibilities for growth in human strength

and self-confidence as a result of appropriate identification. But who can identify with the Rev. Mr. Perfect, or the Rev. Ms. Unknown? Ministers who hide themselves as persons rob people of these needed identifications. It also increases the sense of separation between the congregation and the minister. It teaches alienation and encourages the impersonal in the midst of a style of contemporary life where the gospel claim upon us is that of reconciliation, communion, and personalizing.

The necessary and facilitating communication of empathy reaches its limits if self-disclosure is not included at a later point in the processes of counseling and preaching, and may even add to the people's feelings of frustration. "The minister seems to know, or even understand *my* problems and pains and conflicts and doubts, but how can he (or she) help me out of my distress or despair and toward growth in the faith when he (or she) is so far removed from such humanity as mine?"

A minister and teacher, speaking to seminary students, once declared that he got the most positive response to his preaching when he shared his doubts and fears rather than when he proclaimed his faith. It seems to me that speaking *only* in these terms would reach a point of diminishing returns, perhaps even a point of damage, since preaching *is* proclaiming a *faith.* The important point though, is that doubts and fears and temptations and depression and anger and mixed motivation are the realistic context of our faith, and proclaiming *my* faith accurately also includes its context, which makes my faith pertinent and meaningful and even more powerful for me.

People must have for their own growth, for the meeting of their needs, not someone telling them what "*the* faith" is in a vacuum, but who those of us who are proclaiming *our* faith actually are as human beings. We ministers all too often seem to be afraid that it will be damaging to people if they know us as human beings. What then does this fear really communicate concerning our feelings about ourselves, and about our respect for other persons?

In fact, faith can be meaningful and growth-producing for others only if they know *our* humanity. It must be emphasized, however, that this self-disclosure must be quite selective in preaching as well as in counseling. It must be offered in terms of its helpfulness to the others, and not initiated by the kind of emotional and problem-centered exhibitionism that gives us, the preachers, something of the very temporary exhilaration of any exhibitionist, and which is repeatedly and even compulsively indulged in only for our own sakes.

Such self-disclosure may be regularly but also sensitively and appropriately conveyed in many ways, some of which may sound something like:

"Some of you have raised a question about . . . and frankly I've often wondered about that myself."
"I remember the great surge of anxiety I felt when I (or my wife, or child) was about to go into surgery."
"I once had an experience in which. . . . "
"And when he said that, I was absolutely furious."
"There was a time when we were confronted with that problem in our family, and I just didn't seem to know how to handle it, and we decided to . . . ."

If the church is not the *honest* community, it is no *community* at all. If the pastor is not the model of genuineness and self-disclosure, then upon whom may we depend to guide and empower the community of faith in the direction of the honesty that we must have with each other and before God? If we cannot know and be known in the church, how can we hear, "Your sins are forgiven. Take up your bed and go home " (Matthew 9:6). Someone needs to be able to say *for* the congregation *in the midst of the* congregation, "This is who we really are!" "And how are they to hear without a preacher?" (Romans 10:14).

Confrontation

The sixth facilitative condition is confrontation.[16] According to Carkhuff's definition, confrontation is neither verbal shock treatment nor accusations nor harshness nor punishing types of statements. In preaching it would not be measured by an increase in decibels. It may in fact be very soft and very tentative. The assumption is that a person needs and—way down underneath some amount of resistance and defense, even wants—undistorted, external observation and evaluation of his or her behavior. When this type of observation and evaluation is made by a perceptive observer, it can be growth-producing. Clinebell states very clearly that the condition for growth is confrontation in the context of caring.[17] Confrontation is defined very precisely in terms of discrepancies which we perceive in the other person, and, in counseling, pointing up these discrepancies through direct and indirect questioning as well as through reflective statements.

There may be a discrepancy, for example, between *what* another person says and *how* he or she says it: "I hear you talking about being very angry, but I don't sense any expression of the anger itself. What sort of feelings are you actually aware of right at this moment?" A second type of discrepancy is between the other person's insights and actions, or between the person's stated goals and his or her actions: "I guess what you're saying and doing doesn't make much sense to me. You say that you want to do this so you may end up in a particular position and yet you seem to be taking steps that lead inevitably in another direction. Are you aware of this? What do you suppose is going on here?" A third type of discrepancy is between the other person's experience of himself or herself and the helper's perception of that person: "You continue to talk about yourself in terms of being a failure, but when I look at the way in which you actually perform, your feelings about yourself are quite different from the situation which I observe."

In preaching as in counseling, confrontation is clearly most effective when it is based upon one's own actual observations of the other person's behavior, that is, when it is clearly tied to a reality to which we can point. In this way, we are not caught in the destructive trap of passing judgment on the other. We are simply pointing up reality as we observe it. Thus, confrontation in preaching is not a verbal slap in the face in terms of its intent, although it may be experienced as such by some people. It is not condemnation of the other person, or of his or her behavior. That is God's responsibility. It is not venting our anger on another person—although, realistically, there are times when we *are* legitimately angry. If we are, we should recognize it, say so clearly, and describe concretely what our anger is in response to. This then clears the way for the effective presentation and greater probability of reception of the confrontation which may be involved, so that confrontation becomes not a vehicle for conveying our anger but serves its proper function as a stimulus to the attitudinal and/or behavioral change of the others and provides some guidelines for the nature of the decision-making necessary for such a change.

Confrontation is involved in much of the prophesy of the Old Testament. "If you do *this,* then *that* will happen." "You *say* you worship Yahweh, but you *do* something else." Or, Nathan to David, "You agree that this man acted unfairly in the situation described, yet you have acted precisely the same way."

Confrontation as an essential ingredient of the verbal helping relationship, an obvious facilitative condition of pastoral care, makes quite clear the fact that there is no conflict between "pastoral" and "prophetic" preaching, since confrontation itself is a necessary element in both. Confrontation is properly an expression of love, because it seeks to bring people into touch with the reality of their own beings, bringing them into greater internal harmony with themselves, with the social realities in which we live, and with the reality of God himself.

Immediacy

The final facilitative condition of a helping relationship is immediacy.[18] Immediacy refers to how both persons are experiencing the relationship between them, and particularly the willingness on the part of the helping person to utilize the present relationship—right here, right now, what is taking place right at this moment between us—to help the other person understand his or her own feelings and behavior, and then to express himself or herself in regard to them. This requires a great deal of sensitivity, since the helping person must recognize expressions on the part of the other that in various disguised forms might be referring to the relationship between the two of them. For example, a member of your congregation with whom you have been engaged in a number of ways now seeks you out for help and the two of you have begun to talk. You now hear that person beginning to be very critical of other ministers, and you hear something like the following: "Oh, these ministers. They like all the attention *they* get, but they never really have time to pay attention to anyone else." Empathy alone might lead us to respond something like "I can hear a great deal of irritation in your voice when you talk about those who don't pay proper attention to you. It's really quite natural to feel mad at someone when you sense that that person who has the opportunity to do so is not really fulfilling your needs." The condition of immediacy, however, would stimulate us to explore even further: "But by talking about ministers as strongly as you are, and recognizing that I'm a minister, I wonder if you might not be reflecting a feeling that you're having right now that *I'm* not paying enough attention to you."

It is not entirely clear to me as to how this condition may be effectively furnished with any regularity in preaching, especially right at the moment that it seems to be called for. One thing we can be sure of, since preaching is an interpersonal process, is that *something* is going on in the people in the congregation. Some may be getting physically tense; some may be frowning; some may be getting very sleepy; some may be withdrawing from us by giving in to fantasy or by outlining the next day's work schedule; some may be shifting uneasily in their seats. How may a minister recognize and refer appropriately to these immediate reactions in order to assist the persons in exploring with greater understanding their own lives? On some occasions he or she may actually refer to what is going on: "I see a number of you smiling (frowning, shaking your heads, etc.). That leads me to think in the light of what I am saying, that . . . (and here follows your interpretation)."

Even when we do not respond verbally in the manner just suggested, it is possible to be aware of people's responses during the sermon. It would then be useful to verify our impressions with a few people during the week, and use the responses derived from the preacher-listener relationship in an appropriate context within the sermon in the next week or two.

These seven ingredients in great amounts and quality must be a part of all relationships which we have with other persons if we want those relationships to be helpful and growth-producing for them as well as fulfilling for ourselves. This has been quite adequately substantiated by psychotherapeutic research and clinical practice. Since preaching, however we may talk about it theologically, is clearly an interpersonal process to which the adjective "helping" can hopefully be applied, the assumption is made that the conditions necessary to elicit deeper self-exploration, increase of insight, motivation to change, evaluation of behavioral alternatives, the facilitation of the decision-making process, and the acting on the basis of those decisions, would be the same, although somewhat differently expressed because of the unique nature of the preacher-congregation relationship. Therefore, the conscious introduction of these conditions into the preaching process would seem to be a necessary precondition for the effective proclamation of the Word of God.

Conclusion

These last two chapters have attempted to bring to bear upon the central ministerial function of preaching some insights from psychology and psychotherapy. These insights shed light, first, on the basic reason for the Hebrew writers' choice of the word "Word" to refer to the acts of God. Their understanding of the dynamic, expressive nature of human words when spoken in the relationship of one person to another, the sharing of one's own self that elicits a response in another, and their experience with the dynamic nature of the acts of God in their own lives and history produced this natural and logical usage. The character of words and how this understanding illuminates the theological concept of the Word, and the relationship of the preacher's words to the time of the expression of the Word of God, were summarized.

Second, with preaching being understood as an interpersonal process, the facilitative conditions of all helping relationships were listed, defined, and to some extent illustrated. An attempt was made to show how these might then be appropriately introduced into sermon preparation and presentation, so that the preacher may, in the most effective way possible, establish through his or her relationship with the congregation an openness to hearing God speak his own Word to his people.

V. The Word in Scripture and Relationship: The Use of the Bible in Pastoral Care

There is something about part of the title of this chapter that immediately strikes a negative note. How am I going to *use* the Bible to help people? This would seem to make the Bible into an instrument to add to our collection of tools, skills, and other resources which we utilize in the helping process. For a member of the community of faith, however, the Bible is not merely a usable object, a tool. It is the story of how we came into being as a people of God, the record of people's response to their experience of God's initiative-taking with them, the presentation of Jesus as the Christ, and thus the revelation of who God is in relationship to us. The Bible is also the present, living Word of God to us whenever we open ourselves to his initiative-taking as we read or listen to the words.

However, once this is clearly understood, we must inevitably use words like "use" to talk about the Bible. We use it in our personal devotional life. We use it as the foundation of our preaching. We use it to illustrate and illuminate points in our sermons. How do we use it, then, in our pastoral care and counseling?

Unfortunately, several aspects of our history as a church have combined to produce for some substantial number of people a sense of the "magic" of the Bible. As an object, either whole or in its various parts, it has magical powers. Have it near. Read certain passages. Let it fall open and follow the direction of whatever verse the eye falls upon. Some people seek to use it blindly in this way, and continue to use it so even though it often does not seem to "work," or because it sometimes seems to "work," and all the while missing the power which God seeks to convey through an intelligent reading and prayerful reflection upon its meaning for us. Or, seeking its magic, some people discover that "it" (as an object) fails them, so they angrily discard it, because they know of no other way to tap the resources of God, or otherwise open themselves to God's power and guidance. Therefore, an important avenue to healing and growth is cut off.

As ministers, how are we to use the Bible in an appropriate and effective way with persons in those situations in which we seek to help them, the times of celebration, distress, illness, pain, crises, loss, or emotional disorder? In theological seminary most of us learned little or nothing specifically about how to do this: certainly not in our courses in Bible, and, almost as certainly, not in courses on pastoral care. With three or more years of formal education beyond college, most of us were still left to figure out for ourselves what we were going to do. Usually we ended up using the Bible in one of three ways.

First, because we did not have any clear guidelines, we ignored entirely the possibility that there were constructive ways of bringing biblical literature to bear upon persons' real, immediate life situations. So the Bible was not a part of our pastoral care and counseling at all.

Or, second, we tended to use the Bible in ways that only served to reinforce people's images that it was an "authority," but without their being aware of what sense in which that was true. Therefore, the view of the Bible as a book of magic, or at least borderline magic, without existential meaning, was perpetuated.

Or, third, and probably most of us found ourselves here, we genuinely believed that the Scripture expresses a

Word to us at critical times in our lives, as well as being the long-term foundational source of guidelines for our faith. Therefore, when a person was sick, or in grief, or in some other crisis, we searched out certain passages of scripture that rather obviously were comforting, affirming God's caring, and offering hope. At the end of a pastoral conversation, we would occasionally read a passage that seemed relevant, and then conclude with prayer.

In the light of the centrality of the Bible to our life of faith, the first approach is quite unsatisfactory. In the light of the reality of the potential meaningfulness and power of the scripture, the second application of the Bible is actually damaging. The third alternative is quite legitimate, but also insufficient and limited if it is used alone.

Our questions, then, are: "What are the ways in which we may more adequately draw upon this central resource of and stimulus to faith within the context of those functions of ministry which we designate by the term pastoral care, including pastoral counseling? What are those situations of pastoral care which lend themselves most readily to the Word of the scripture?" An approach to responding to these questions may be guided by a brief look at some of those contributions of psychotherapy which might help us identify some of the functional principles.

The Bible, Psychotherapy, and Pastoral Care

The title of this section is both general and clumsy. The specific designation, however, would be even clumsier, something like "Insights of the Bible Itself which Psychotherapy Apart from the Bible Explicitly Affirms and Utilizes, and which then Relate to the Use of the Bible in Pastoral Care."

To go at the subject this way is unfortunately made necessary by the way in which so many people, including many of us ministers, pay attention to the Bible as the Word of *God.* It is this, of course, to the person of faith. We look there for his Word to us. That is, as we read or listen to its words, we anticipate God's speaking his Word to us. Especially, we ministers utilize the Bible as both the foundation of our preaching and as a primary source for sermon illustration. In so doing, unfortunately we are all too prone to overlook the thoroughly representative humanness of it. The reason it can be *God's* Word to us is because it accurately describes us in so many different forms: it portrays our behavior, reveals our inner thoughts and desires, asks our questions, uncovers our defenses, acts out our conflicts and ambivalence, mirrors our ways of relating to one another, shows our idolatry, opens up "the grandeur and misery" of us all for all of us to see, identifies our strengths and weaknesses, and reflects the ways in which we communicate and befuddle communication. It is our story. In the infinite combination of its parts, it is our life.

Contemporary psychotherapy also refers to our life's story, in some ways similar to and in other ways quite different from the Bible. Quite obviously the purpose of psychotherapy is not to tell the story of the community of faith, with many different literary forms moving back and forth between the presentation of the people's search for God and God's initiative in dealing with his people. But apart from this, it does describe in a thoroughgoing manner the inner depths of human life, the complexity of human relationships, the scope of human problems, the dynamics which sometimes energize and sometimes paralyze us; and, in a systematic manner, psychotherapy provides an operational approach to the loosening of the forces which keep us in human bondage and a method of assisting us in increasing our powers of responsible decision-making and behavior.

In one sense, psychotherapy has not discovered anything totally new about persons. The range of human problems, unconscious inner forces, family dynamics, destructive relationships, however these may be spelled out by different schools of psychotherapy, can all be illustrated with biblical material, as well as the great literature from many nations, many peoples, and many periods of history. Psychotherapy has, however, in its practice which results in the healing of human ills and in personal (or marriage or family) growth, described us in all of our intra- and interpersonal complexity, given us an alternative language which can be useful in its descriptive nature, and has shed new light both on the reasons for human distress and maladaptive behavior and on methods of relieving distress and effecting change. Neither the language of psychotherapy nor its descriptions of human behavior nor its therapeutic methods should be thought of as competitive with the Judeo-Christian view of persons and our life together. Both the psychological and theological views of the person are valid perspectives, and they offer enlightening ways of discovering human life and its meaning. They may overlap at points and may be complementary at others. Of course, all psychological descriptions are not necessarily equally valid, just as all theological statements are not equally valid. This is the reason that both psychologists and theologians continue their research and their debates among themselves as they seek to test, clarify, and revise their points of view. But the debate is as much, if not more, *within* each field as it is *between* the disciplines. Therefore, it is quite appropriate that we look at some of the emphases of contemporary psychotherapy which might focus our attention on particular ways of utilizing the Bible in supporting and assisting the growth of persons in those situations which call for pastoral care.

The first of these is what Theodore Reik calls "listening with the third ear," an expression which he borrowed from Nietzsche.[1] This expression refers to a quality of listening to and observing a person which considers the whole human being (conscious and unconscious), paying attention to a variety of forms and purposes of human communication, both verbal and nonverbal. It is the attempt to receive the *whole* message, and not just the literal meaning of the words which the person uses. In order to accomplish this it also pays attention to the inner reactions of the therapist. It attends to the tone of voice, pace of speech, and rise or fall in volume of the person speaking. It observes posture, eyes, bodily movement, what the hands are doing, and changes in facial coloration. It is aware of the selective nature of our speech, the fact that we may say some things and not others, both consciously and unconsciously, and therefore hears what is *not* said as well as what is spoken. It accepts the truth that at times we use language with the intent to reveal ourselves, at other times to cover up the truth about ourselves, and that on occasion we do both at the same time. It understands that we may use some forms of speech to say very important things about ourselves, although on the surface of it the language does not seem to be communicating that much about us at all. Listening with the third ear focuses especially on the emotions which accompany the verbal expression, whether what we say is explicitly talking about feelings or not. Finally, at least for this discussion, listening with the third ear takes into account the forms of verbal and nonverbal behavior which are communicating the other person's response to authority or relationship with authority figures, with typical forms of speech and other behavior toward authorities being utilized as an ingredient of their relationship with us, the therapist or the pastor or, in our case, the church and the Bible itself.

None of these elements which make up the type and quality of listening which is necessary for effective psychotherapy are "new under the sun," but in their totality they have been self-consciously developed in a systematic manner so that listening in this way and responding verbally in keeping with these elements may properly be thought of both as a science and as an art.

It is quite obvious that this quality of listening and responding in appropriate ways which reflect such listening is essential for effective pastoral care. It always has been so. Increasingly, methods of training in these forms of listening and communicating are being developed and utilized as a part of the total education of ministers. In addition, though, the point of this discussion is that all these elements of listening with the third ear may guide us in the effective use of the Bible in our pastoral care work. The major part of this chapter is intended to illustrate this use to clarify a person's feelings, conflicts, perspectives, values, and relationships, and to guide and empower the person in his or her personal, marriage, family, emotional, and spiritual growth.

Another major emphasis of contemporary psychotherapy is the indisputable evidence confirming the power of the emotional life, both those feelings of which we are consciously aware and those which operate to influence our behavior but which remain unconscious to us, and the power of unconscious conflicts and desires to initiate and shape behavior and relationships. This would make it imperative that we never be satisfied with a use of the Bible which focuses only on its rational use, which stays on the level of intellectual discussion, or which simply gives "biblical answers" in some literalistic sense. At whatever point biblical material is introduced into the pastoral conversation, whether by parishioner or minister, for whatever expressed reason, the minister must always be alert to the affective area of the person's life which needs to be explored in order for the Bible to have its full impact upon the life of the person.

Along with the power of the emotional life and of unconscious conflicts and desires to influence behavior, psychotherapy also recognizes the importance of the cognitive process, the need to think clearly and with a minimum of distortion, and a person's needs for information as a part of the material which provides the basis for clarifying one's thinking, for more appropriate and responsible decision-making, and for the developing of meaning. One should also keep in mind the interaction between the emotions and the rational thought processes.

Finally, as a methodology, psychotherapy emphasizes the necessity of a person's thorough exploration of his or her personal situation (one's inner life, relationships, values, etc.), of the resources available to one, and of various perspectives, interpretations, and alternatives. This recommends to us ministers a procedure which suggests that we not be too eager to give, as referred to before, "the biblical answer" to a person's condition or situation, but that we work patiently with the person in facilitating his or her process of self-exploration, and that biblical materials be used as a part of the exploration as much as they are a part of the problem-solving.

While a long term psychotherapeutic procedure in its detail is far more complex than this discussion reveals, these emphases referred to here furnish significant suggestions concerning the minister's use of the Bible in pastoral care.

The Use of the Bible in Pastoral Care

People's Questions about the Bible

It is not unusual for persons occasionally to raise with ministers questions which sound like, "What does the Bible say about . . . ?" Or, "When Jesus (or Paul or whoever) said, '. . . ,' what do you think is meant by this?" You can fill in the blanks from your own experience. Such questions may very often be a particular form of a person's asking for a pastoral conversation. We should always be alert to this possibility. We need to keep our "third ear" on duty as much as possible. It has been my experience that people are rarely interested in a particular passage or what the Bible says about a specific issue or problem from a purely detached intellectual standpoint or idle curiosity. A central question to keep in mind is, "Why is this person raising *this* question *now?"* Part of our task is to explore this question in response to biblical issues people raise with us.

There are a variety of ways of responding to this situation that may facilitate an exploration of what might be going on in the life of the questioner. About the only way to squelch such exploration is to play the role of biblical authority. "You have asked this question. My answer is . . .," or, "The Bible clearly states that . . .," and that is the end of it.

Usually the very simple question, "Why do you ask?" will open the floodgates of a story that with little or no further assistance will pour out, accompanied by a variety of emotions. Then we may move very quickly into the same type of pastoral conversation or even counseling that would have been initiated if the person had come and simply laid out a clearly delineated problem before us.

Occasionally, of course, a person will answer in a

noncommittal manner, "Oh, I was just curious." Then the minister might follow with something like, "You know, I've discovered that most curiosity is not idle, and that usually something is going on in a person's life which leads to an interest in a particular passage or what the Bible says about a particular issue. I wonder if you are aware of what this might be for you." Of course, this type of response needs to be made in a way which is sensitive to the feelings of the other person. We certainly need to avoid being too coy or evasive concerning the question or too invasive of the other person's life. We must be open to the possibility that there is no deep or mysterious problem involved. We may even choose not to respond along the line suggested. Nevertheless, even if not spoken immediately, words such as these frequently point to the importance of attempting to discover something about the situation of the person who is raising the question. "What is the unpardonable sin? What does the Bible say about divorce or homosexuality? What did Jesus mean when he said that to lust after a woman is committing adultery in one's heart?" These questions and many others like them probably reflect a persons's questions about himself or herself, about one's own situation or condition or feelings, or about one's concern for someone else. Obviously, if after the minister has sought with sensitivity to elicit a personal response, then the scripture may be discussed with the person in such a way that accurate information is given and an interpretation or relevant alternative interpretations may be raised. Hopefully, the minister would do this in a manner that would invite further discussion at a later time.

This goal might be accomplished, first, by seeking to elicit from the person where he or she is in regard to the issue at the present time. "Before I respond to your question, I wonder what you have already been thinking about this yourself. How has your mind been grappling with it? How does it strike you? What interpretations do *you* see as possibilities?" Then the minister might go on to reinforce some responses and perhaps raise questions about others by sharing with the person the way in which certain basic principles of biblical interpretation (such as seeking to discover the historical setting of the passage, trying to find the most accurate translation of the original language, reading the entire context, reading alternative modern translations, and searching out other related passages) may enlighten our quest for understanding. Then the minister asks for feedback: "Does this make sense to you?" Or, "How do you respond to this?"

At all times we must be attentive to the person's feelings as we are moving through the different phases of our discussion, but never hesitating to offer the informational, cognitive input that is relevant to the issue.

People's Use of Religious Language

Some number of people will use biblical and/or other language of faith to support certain personal attitudes or positions or behavior, as a defense of some kind, or as a way of saying certain important things about themselves and their experiences. A sensitive and skillful minister will be able to be patient in his or her exploration with such persons in attempting to pin down with some clarity how it is they are using religious language, what meanings they are seeking to express, what unrealistic distortions they are seeking to support, and then use an intelligent exegesis of the Bible both to bring a new understanding to them and their situation as well as the authority of the Bible to support that new understanding.

Joe had led a rough and occasionally violent life for years. He was also alcoholic. Recently he had undergone a conversion experience and was now openly a Christian.

His problems were not automatically solved, however, and under pressure he went to a psychiatrist. He used the language of faith constantly, interspersed with frequent references to the Bible, and even biblical quotations as a way of expressing himself on any issue. Facing the increasing frustration of what he experienced as a smoke screen, the psychiatrist told Joe not even to talk to him anymore in that language, and referred Joe to a minister for consultation.

The minister began very slowly, looking for a way to relate positively to Joe, asking about his feelings about seeing the minister. Joe was somewhat surprised at this but answered honestly that he did feel under pressure and, in fact, felt rather anxious about it. He seemed to suspect that by trying to change his language the psychiatrist was attempting to take away his faith and that the minister may very well be a party to the plot. The minister had empathy for his feelings and remarked that he would undoubtedly feel some anger and apprehension under the same circumstances. This helped considerably in reducing some of Joe's resistance to having been put on the spot in being referred to the minister. However, in the conversation that immediately followed, Joe's statements tended to be a rather aggressive proclamation of his beliefs, almost as if he were expecting or even inviting rejection. The minister, however, did not challenge him at all, but rather continued to express interest in Joe's faith and the role which his faith played in his life, affirming the validity of Christian experience and its importance, and the use of the language of faith to describe not only that experience but other approaches to one's life situation. However, very persistently, time after time, when Joe would use theological terms or quote from the Bible, the minister would ask him what he meant by the term, or what he was seeking to express about his own life by the use of the word or words, or to expand upon the meaning of the Bible verse, clearly stating each time that this was in service of the minister's attempt to understand him. The implicit communication to Joe was always, "I am taking you, your Christian faith, your language, and your problems very seriously. I will work to get to know and understand you."

The minister's tentative hypothesis was that Joe was still plagued by guilt and insecurity, that the seemingly closed nature of his belief system was an attempt to fend off the pain of these feelings, and perhaps even using his language in such a stereotyped way as a means of keeping other people at a distance in order to avoid personal involvement with them and thus protect himself.

As additional conversations were held and the minister continued in a patient and persistent manner to ask for the meaning to Joe of the language and biblical quotations, Joe began to demonstrate that he could express his needs in everyday language, needs growing out of his own childhood and family relationships, the need for a reliable, caring "Father," a sense of personal worth, and a hope that ultimately things would be all right for him.

At one point he talked about his inflexible opposition to his wife's working at a job outside of the home, and gave a biblical warrant for his position. When asked what passage in the Bible he was referring to, he replied that it was Ephesians 5. The minister responded that he could not remember that this explicitly prohibited a wife's working. Joe reluctantly agreed, but went on to say that Ephesians declared the husband to be the head of the house, and that since he did not want his wife to work, therefore she should not. This set the agenda: an exploration of the source of his opposition to his wife's working. It was naturally assumed that since the Bible did not explicitly prohibit it his opposition came out of some particular needs of his own or had something to do with the relationship between him and his wife. In other words, what did his wife's working mean to him? When some clarity could be gained about this matter then a discussion of the actual meaning of the passage of scripture he referred to would be appropriate.

With his view of the Bible as being the verbally and literally inspired Word of God, it seemed to be useful to start at this point, rather than making the direct move into a discussion of his present needs and his relationship with his wife, which he would probably have resisted if approached that way. The minister opened the bible and read, "Wives, be subject to your husbands, as to the Lord" (Ephesians 5:22). What does this mean? Joe's response was that he as the husband was to be obeyed by his wife, and she was disobeying him by working. But the minister then read further: "Husbands should love their wives as their own bodies" (Ephesians 5:28). So what does that mean? Joe knew. His wife was to be considered and her needs attended to. In the discussion that followed Joe agreed that what the whole passage is referring to (in addition to presenting an analogy of Christ's relationship to the church), is a relationship in marriage which is a *two*-way, not a *one*-way, street.

What, then, would that mean for him and his wife? What was the meaning of her working? For Joe, it meant that her dependence upon him was reduced, increasing his insecurity, diminishing his sense of his own worth as a man, man the provider. But because the scripture was pointing to working out the details of a relationship in which there was to be mutuality, he committed himself to this task, clearly the necessary task before him.

What took place in this pastoral counseling process (three interviews) was the beginning clarification to Joe of the real meaning of his faith and its language for him at the present and a decrease of the rigid and even defensive manner of using the language of faith, both of these combining to open up the possibility of a growth in faith that had actually been closed off before. Even though faith initially may have meaning to us, a distortion of faith and our misuse of faith then stands in the way of the growth of faith. Joe, because of his own intense needs, had distorted his interpretation of the scripture; but, through the use of the scripture itself, he was enabled to focus on these needs and on his relationship with his wife so that effective work on that relationship could be initiated.

Another example of the use of the Bible itself to combat the misuse of the language of faith, to enable a person to identify his own genuine needs (and the strength of those needs), and to open a person to the possibility of genuine growth in faith is provided by Sam, a young man who was telling his minister of occasions when he had been visited by the Holy Spirit. One of these involved the smoking of marijuana and intense sexual arousal. He described the ecstatic nature of the experience, and how good it made him feel. He pointed to this as being validating for the explicit religious interpretations he placed upon so many of his other experiences and supporting his interest in thinking and talking about religion, with the implication being that if he could only have available at all times the power of the experience that he described, all of his many problems could be resolved. After encouraging a full description of the experience itself and the feelings which accompanied it and the present feelings he was having as he was telling about it, the minister, who already had a firm relationship with him, very clearly said that it certainly could be understood how this occasion had been experienced by Sam as so exciting and powerful. The smoking of pot reduced the considerable anxiety that influenced so much of what he did, and it produced a feeling of well-being. Also, most people have had feelings of ecstasy related to intense sexual desire and the fantasies of satisfaction similar to those which Sam had been having. However, the minister went on, when the Bible speaks of the Holy Spirit, it is not referring primarily to good feelings, and, to the extent that good feelings might be present in an experience of the Holy Spirit, they are secondary to other factors. Rather, Paul identifies the Holy Spirit with the spirit of Christ, which links the Holy Spirit with the observable life and the impact of the life, death, and resurrection of Jesus. So an experience of the Holy Spirit properly has the influence of forming within one the mind of Christ, continued education in the faith, participation in the community of faith, and guidance in one's behavior, characterized by responsibility toward oneself and a caring for others which expresses itself in concrete and appropriate action. Because of the authority which Sam attributed to the Bible, it was possible for him to give up his need to talk about that experience in terms of the Holy Spirit, which really had the effect of blocking the continuing work of the Spirit in constructive ways in his own life.

In this section we have sought to illustrate that people use religious language and biblical material to reveal something about themselves. On other occasions the message may be distorted by the intensity of one's personal needs. In either or a combination of both instances, the Bible itself may be used to help a person identify his or her needs, thereby clearing the way for more accurate perspectives on the biblical message to the person with those particular needs, thus leading to growth in Christian faith, which would include emotional growth and the improvement of one's significant relationships.

Personal Issues Which Relate to Biblical Teaching

For every person, Christian or non-Christian, there are times of emotional crisis, disturbed or disrupted relationships, extremely difficult problems, or issues of personal behavior. Some Christian people will at these times look at the Bible for help and find it in a realistic and positive way, but others will find passages which they experience as being even more disturbing for themselves. Still others refer to some scripture as supporting their feelings, attitudes, or behavior in ways which seem to hinder growth. The latter two situations are the ones which this section will deal with and illustrate. It certainly should not be assumed that any of the foregoing words mean that it is a "problem" to be solved every time some aspect of the biblical message disturbs us. As a matter of fact, if we can actually read the Bible and remain unperturbed then this may be a reflection of our total insensitivity to its message and to the power of God himself. However, all of us are well-acquainted with instances in which people seem to be disturbed by passages that most others do not find so distressing. The degree of their reaction seems to be out of keeping with the reality of the situation, or their misreading of scripture leads to distorted or inappropriate responses. The following discussion will attempt to show how the insights of psychotherapy, an appreciation of the lively, dynamic nature of the Bible, and responsible exegesis may be combined to assist people in dealing with their feelings of distress or in changing behavior which is inappropriate or even maladaptive and at least in some sense a barrier to their personal growth, including their growth in faith.

A woman had a very bad marriage of some twenty years. Her huband was quite caught up in his work; he was not a very giving person emotionally; his wife's schemes to pressure him into giving aroused more and more resentment and resistance on his part, leading him to alternate between increased withdrawal and quite abusive behavior, resulting in increased frustration and even fear on the part of the wife. After an attempt at marriage counseling, and after years of considering some action, she filed for a divorce. Now she was wanting to talk with her minister about the great guilt she was experiencing since "the Bible forbids divorce except in cases of adultery, and he hasn't done that." So she was wanting to talk about the Bible and divorce, a very legitimate request and one which appears on the surface to have a very appropriate connection between the feelings she was having and a biblical standard which the church has in different ways over the centuries sought to take quite seriously.

Of course, with her taking literally the Matthew passage as she remembered it and attributing her guilt to disobeying Jesus' "command" about divorce (Matthew 19:3-9), she was only setting herself up for the worse shock of discovering that Mark, which probably contains what is closer to the words Jesus actually spoke, does not make even infidelity an exception (Mark 10:2-12). Naturally, the skillful minister will not introduce this unpleasant biblical reality until other preliminary work has been accomplished and the person is actually at a point of being capable of grappling effectively with the biblical materials.

It is always important in dealing with a person who feels guilt over disobedience to some biblical injunction to discover why it is he or she attributes more power to the "command" passages than to the "forgiveness" passages. People so often seem to believe the one but not the other. There are not usually absolutely rational reasons for this selective response (although certainly there are occasions of ignorance of the existence of certain passages, but surely *not* of the many Old Testament references to forgiveness and Jesus' frequent assurances). Therefore, we must take time with a person to explore the source of the affective power of the guilt he or she is experiencing.

The minister encouraged this woman to talk about her marriage relationship in detail, how it had deteriorated over the years, how she had suffered in it, how she set herself up to be abused, but also how she had experienced her husband's abusing her. The question was raised as to whether she thought that God's will for her was to spend the rest of her life in an unhappy, destructive relationship:

"No, not really."

"Then you're feeling guilty over making some decision for your life that you genuinely believe is the most constructive one for you under the circumstances. That doesn't seem to fit, does it?" "No, it doesn't."

Then the minister, using both his observation of the manner in which she described her husband's behavior, the words and tone of voice, and his basic knowledge of human reactions to suggest that it sounded as if she were really very angry at her husband. This was difficult for her to admit; but with additional description of her relationship, with encouragement from the minister that it is very normal to get mad when people frustrate and abuse us, she began to be more and more expressive of the great amount of fury she had harbored for years. However, over the past few months, she had become aware of that anger, and on the basis of it acted to initiate the divorce. In the conversation, it began to be clear that she was feeling guilty, *not* primarily over the divorce, but over the anger itself, which she had from her earliest years been taught was fearful, destructive, and sinful.

Now a major task presented iself. She needed to begin to grow accustomed to the idea that anger is a normal reaction under many circumstances, that the *feeling* of anger is not prohibited by the Bible, and that the capacity for anger is a gift from God as a source of energy to be used in constructive ways, and that Jesus himself got angry on a number of occasions. The Bible was explicitly used to assist this process. Then it seemed to be useful to move back to the issue of divorce itself. The point which is clearly being made in both Mark and Matthew is that God's primary will for persons is a fulfilling permanent marriage. The major purpose of the passage is not primarily to say that divorce is forbidden, but that a marriage which is mutually satisfying to husband and wife is God's purpose. The meaning is clear: divorce is contrary to the *primary* will of God To *this* there are no exceptions. However, the whole Bible is realistic concerning who we people are. Even Christians are still fully human beings who, in our anxiety and insecurity and grasping for the answers to our situation, defend and distort and attack and hurt in many ways. In this kind of life there is not always happiness and fulfillment in marriage, and in fact, people divorce. Therefore, sin is involved in divorce, as it is involved in so much of our behavior and so many of our relationships. But the New Testament is not just a new set of laws. Rather, it is the gospel, and the one who made the statement about God's will for marriage and about divorce is also the one who represented God's forgiveness in his forgiving people time and time again. These statements concerning the availability and the power of forgiveness are to be taken just as seriously as those concerning the primary will of God.

This woman illustrates several issues. First, this interaction is an example of the care we must always take to explore in detail the situation which the person is bringing to us rather than immediately answering the questions they raise with us. We "listen with the third ear" rather than follow the immediate direction of the person's words. This woman demonstrates a reaction which is a common one for most of us at one time or another, the attributing of an emotion to some cause other than the one which originally gave rise to it. With this woman, if we had sought to deal with the guilt over divorce, her guilt could not have been fully and constructively handled, since certainly most of her guilt seemed actually to be connected with her anger.

Second, and this is really an elaboration of the first point, this situation clearly demonstrates the importance of not moving too quickly into a rational intellectual discussion of the biblical material. The emotions need to be identified and expressed in the context of a discussion of the entire situation before the more thorough work with the scripture itself can be accomplished most effectively.

Third, this situation illustrates the explicit use of biblical materials as supportive of the type of change that a person needs in order to get rid of handicapping feelings, to lead one into a more constructive resolution of the present problem, and to introduce a new perspective which may assist a person in meeting future situations in which similar reactions might be involved. Not only are some basic feelings reeducated, but the person is educated in a method of dealing with the scripture which opens the door to a much deeper meaning to the person of the Bible and its real resources, thus contributing significantly to potential growth in faith.

A second example not only illustrates these same procedures, but points to an additional insight which psychotherapy urges us to keep in mind concerning the effective helping process. This is the principle of selectivity. What do people talk about, and what do they fail to bring up for discussion? What do they emphasize and what do they minimize?

What psychologists refer to as projective techniques of psychological evaluation are based on this principle. The Rorschach test is a common one. It is comprised of a series of ten ink blots, forms which obviously have no message and which tell no story. A person is merely to describe what he or she sees. No person can describe it all (or if one tries to, that certainly tells us something about the person, too). So people select parts or shapes or, for a few of the cards, colors. Even though there are a number of rather common and frequent responses, people also differ. They respond to certain things and fail to respond to others on the basis of their past experiences, conflicts, repressed emotions, forgotten experiences, and present needs.

In fact, and this is the point, we respond to everything and everybody to some extent in the same way. It is hardly surprising, then, that we find ourselves reacting to the Bible in this manner, and even less surprising when we remember the Bible's accurate portrayal of the human condition and every aspect of human life and experience. Why is it that a person who feels guilty over getting angry, can go to a very few and usually somewhat ambiguous verses that to him or her suggest that anger is bad, and completely overlook and fail to deal with the fact of Jesus' anger? Why does another person use a verse about this or that act or attitude to continue to castigate themselves and support his or her persistent guilt, and not experience the relevance of the pervading biblical theme of God's forgiveness? Or how is it that some do just the opposite, making forgiveness the entire message and failing to hear any radical call to responsible behavior? Why do we *all* take one passage seriously, and pay no attention at all to others? This is a question which we need to raise with ourselves for growth in our own Christian lives as well as with others as we act as their pastors.

A minister had been talking with Joan in regard to feelings of guilt and fear—even to the point of panic—when she attended church. These are reactions to church attendance which either separately or together are more common than we ordinarily think. The feelings began not long after the death of her son. The factors involved were numerous and complex, but it is enough for our introduction to her situation here to say that church attendance itself became counterproductive to her growth in faith as a result of these strong reactions, and yet she was very much afraid of what might happen if she stopped attending church altogether.

One day she appeared for her counseling session very angry. The following Sunday there was to be a woman minister officiating and preaching at her church, and she was under considerable pressure to attend in spite of the fact that she did not want to do so at all. In fact, in the terms in which she framed it, it was not just that she did not want to, but that it was actually a moral issue with her. She felt that she would be doing something wrong by participating in that service, since, she said, the Bible prohibited women from taking a leadership role in church services.

Now, how would a minister most helpfully deal with her response to this situation? Naturally, it would depend somewhat, although not entirely, upon whether the minister agrees or disagrees with her about women's "keeping silent in the church." Even agreement with her, however, would not basically alter the procedure if we keep in mind our responsibility to assist persons in exploring their own feelings, responses, values, situations, and to use the Bible itself both to assist in this exploration and give guidelines as to commitments and behavior.

In other words, to respond immediately by supporting

her position through the use of the Bible or to try to help her see where she is "wrong" in her position by the use of competent exegesis would miss the opportunity to lead her into significant growth. Consider a response something like the following: "As you've described the situation it's very clear to me that you have a great amount of feeling about a woman's preaching and the 'wrongness' of your attendance on that day. I wonder if you always react with this intensity of feeling to *all* of the biblical injunctions." Something like this is a guaranteed stopper. After the first pause, the only answer any honest person can give is, "No." Nobody reacts with the same intensity of feeling and degree of commitment to all of the biblical injunctions.

The next line is to continue, "Then I wonder if you are aware of why it is that this particular verse (or verses or whatever) means so much to you and elicits such a strong response?" Some people may very quickly be able to tell about some experience or relationship or set of circumstances out of which the conviction arises. If they cannot, we may then go on to say something like, "It's been my experience that when we have considerable conviction about certain issues and much less feeling about others, there's usually a reason, and this frequently ties into some early experience of ours. Perhaps if we can explore this together we might be able to discover what this is for you. This process might prove to be very useful to you in your growth in the Christian life."

With Joan, the obvious thing to begin with was the question of "women ministers." "What does this mean to you? Have you actually had experiences with women ministers before?" She herself was startled at the realization that she had not thought of this on her own. It was something she had blocked out of her memory. However, with the minister's merely raising that issue aloud she remembered very well. When Joan was twelve years old, her mother joined a Pentecostal church in which women preachers were common. Her mother forced her to attend services, and Joan found herself very frightened by the loud emotional sermons and the variety of open emotional reactions on the part of the people in the congregation. She was also afraid not to go because of her mother's threats.

In addition, the church itself seemed to drive a wedge between mother and daughter in yet another way, since the mother spent so much time and emotional energy with church activities precisely at a time when a daughter needs to be drawing close to her mother in ways that encourage positive identifications.

As Joan remembered and talked about all that had gone on in her early adolescence, her fears were rekindled and expressed, and her anger at her mother and the women preachers began to be felt all over again, and these were discussed. She very clearly recognized as the conversation went on that these fearful and angry experiences related to mother and church ("Mother Church") were the source of the potency of her feelings concerning the woman preacher who was coming Sunday, and exacerbated her reaction to being under pressure to attend.

This illustration clearly points out that powerful feelings often have to be dealt with at an early stage in discussing biblical materials, theological statements, ethical issues, and Christian commitments. If they are not identified, expressed, and fully explored, then the other stages of the helping process will not take effect. However, *just* to deal with the feelings and their source and to work to diminish their intensity (or even occasionally get rid of them) when they are inappropriate to the present situation, is only to get rid of a road block, and therefore is by itself insufficient. In the situation with

Joan, she was still left with the basic question for herself as to whether it is all right or not all right for a woman to function as a minister, or, more personally, for her to attend worship when it is led by a woman. It was no longer such a burning issue to her, but the question, of course, can still be raised. So once again it is important to go to the Bible itself.

Joan, of course, had in mind passages such as I Corinthians 14:33-35 and 1 Timothy 2:11-12. Without much question, these two statements are very explicit about women's silence and their yielding authority to men in the church. In the conversation with Joan, however, the minister had the opportunity to introduce her to some new procedures in utilizing the Bible as a method of educating her Christian faith and guiding her behavior. While these two passages mentioned above are very explicit, they are also in considerable contrast with I Corinthians 11:5, 11-13. Verse 5 clearly assumes that women will be praying in the church, and verses 11 and 12 refer to the interdependence of men and women, of their equal need for one another, and to the foundation of all relationships within the church, specifically that all of us, male and female, are from God. In addition, the "women keep silent" passages are in obvious contrast with the rather widespread practice in the early church of women's prominent participation in the church in various ways.

Responsible biblical interpretation does not allow one verse to be used as a proof text against another. Rather the whole picture (verses which agree and verses which disagree) with its historical setting must be examined, evaluated intelligently in the light of the whole context, and all tested by the spirit of Christ, who, in regard to this particular issue under discussion, gave great honor to women.

Such contrasts and conflicts and ambiguities in the text

demand for their best interpretation a person with a somewhat flexible personality, someone with a tolerance for ambiguity, someone with a basic sense of security in the world, someone whose whole faith does not stand on any single biblical text or collection of texts but upon Christ himself.

Joan, with her anger at women in the church and fear of women in the church being greatly diminished, was now free to take a new look at the relevant biblical statements, recognizing that for whatever reason more than one thing is being said, but also recognizing that she has a new freedom in Christ to make a responsible decision concerning her own Christian life after serious consideration of the texts. The result was that she attended the church service with a woman worship leader and preacher, felt neither panic nor anger nor guilt, and, in fact, later reported that the service had meant much to her in terms of her growth as a Christian.

The Bible and the "Mentally Ill"

Most ministers do not often work closely with persons who become seriously "mentally ill," yet almost all ministers are called upon occasionally to help in a situation where a person needs to be taken to a psychiatric hospital, to visit someone in such an institution, or be the pastor to someone who has returned home from the hospital. Because of the intensity of the reaction and the crucial nature of it in the lives of the number of people who are usually involved, it is important for the minister to understand something of what is going on.

It is not the purpose of this section to try to explain the nature of emotional and mental disorder, but merely once again to demonstrate how biblical material may sometimes be used by the severely distressed and confused person and how, at certain stages, the minister may effectively use the Bible itself to help clear up for the person some of the confusion he or she may have, leading him or her into a more constructive use of the scripture in his or her life.

It might be important to point out, however, that the term "mental illness" does not refer to feelings, thought processes, or behavior which are totally different from those all of us are acquainted with in our own lives on an almost daily basis. Most of us know what it is like to feel excited and happy and reasonably self-confident and optimistic on occasions, yet be a bit moody and blue and somewhat pessimistic and have self-doubt at other times. We experience fear and anxiety and guilt, and we deal with these in a variety of ways. We may daydream, withdraw temporarily, rationalize a failure, perform some act of atonement, or get overly busy. Many of us hide at least a few of our angers in different ways. We know what it is to feel confused, forgetting some of the most obvious things. We sometimes do not handle ourselves well in relationships. This account, of course, does not raise the issue of the possibility of physiological factors which may be involved in some disorders, nor the extreme complexity of the psychological origins, but the point being made with regard to the experience and behavior of the emotionally disturbed person as a human being still holds. We have already seen that because of our particular background and our present sense of needs we may go to the Bible and interpret it in a manner which serves us in some way but which is not consistent with the most responsible exegesis and which therefore actually misses the point of the biblical message itself.

The person who is "mentally ill" is in a way simply one of us, only more so. The fear, the sense of threat, is greater. Massive forces of anger are being repressed. The dependence on others is excessive. Confusion and distortion reign. Compulsive behavior overrides rationality and interferes with one's life and relationships. Depression becomes a hopeless black pit of despair, and persistent pessimism may lead to suicidal feelings. In other words, there is a higher degree of intensity, a compulsive nature, a rigid inflexibility, a persistence of certain feelings and ways of thinking, behaving, and relating. Under these circumstances, it is easy to understand that the particular selection and use of biblical material is fragmented, distorted, or highly exaggerated to the point which most people would characterize as "abnormal" at that time.

A psychiatrist reports the case of a teen-age boy who had been a heavy drug user. He was admitted to a state hospital, but the family decided to transfer him to a private hospital for treatment. The mother was driving him from one city to another, but when she stopped for lunch, he asked to remain in the car. When she returned to the car, he shouted, "I have to get my eyeball out!" and he began to gouge his right eye. His mother attempted to stop him, but was unable to do so, and he successfully completed the job. After receiving emergency care for the eye, he was transferred to the psychiatric hospital. There he reported that he had taken some stimulant drug while in the car, and that he then had heard a voice tell him, "If thy right eye offend thee, pluck it out" (Matthew 5:29).[2]

Almost everyone would agree that this is a misuse of the Bible. Even the most confirmed biblical literalists are not all one-eyed. Even they recognize that to take this passage literally does not mean that one should remove the eyeball physically. All of us realize that it is not the eye nor the hand that offends, but our own minds, that particular need we have or believe we have that leads to the feeling and thinking and desiring which is the impetus to behavior that would be offensive in the sense of its irresponsibility to ourselves and/or someone else. Therefore, when a person does what this adolescent did, even though he referred to biblical authority, we all presume that the authority of the Bible is not really what led him to the act. Rather, we assume with good cause that other intense needs are at work in his life to such an extreme degree that the person responds in highly selective and distorted ways to whatever outside sources are available which might in any way relate to these needs. The Bible in our society is one of the most available sources of rich symbolism and, as we have stated, portrays every aspect of human experience. It is not the only one, and deeply disturbed people do not always turn to the Bible. But it is important and available, and many deeply disturbed and confused people, whether they have been related to a religious community or not prior to the time of their disorder, may use it in this pathological manner.

For the most part, because of the intensity of the needs of emotionally disordered persons, the grossly irrational nature of their behavior, and the severity of the distortions, it is not possible to utilize the Bible in a rational way at the outset to attack the basis of the disorder and thus produce healing. It is, of course, sometimes possible to discover what *meaning* their particular use of the Bible has for them at this time, seek to understand their experience of themselves and their world, and respond on that level. A person who is this disordered probably needs hospitalization. At some point in the treatment program, however, when the greatest severity of the disorder begins to be diminished, it is possible to assist many persons to an understanding of the reasons they were using the Bible in the way they were, use a responsible exegesis of the particular material upon which they had focused, as well as other parts of the Bible, to continue to reduce their distortions and increase their sense of reality orientation, and point them to the biblical message which may be a present and realistic source of meaning, strength, and guidance for their lives.

John's home was a fairly typical one in most ways, better off than many financially and culturally. The family was active in the church. John enjoyed success in school academically and in sports and was fairly popular. Before he and his girl friend finished high school, however, she became pregnant by him. Both families would entertain no other solution to the situation than marriage. Neither of the teen-agers (he was 17 and she 16) were ready for marriage, but, "the only way out" prevailed. When the baby arrived, they were even less prepared for parenthood than they were for marriage. In the midst of the many adjustments and the considerable responsibilities they were forced to assume prematurely, they made numerous mistakes. These often resulted in anger, which they handled poorly. As several years went by, behavior patterns developed, especially on John's part, which arose out of anger and in reaction to the intense pressure, and inevitably led to more complex problems in the relationship: fewer needs were adequately met in the marriage, there was more frustration, more anger, in short, a downward spiral of a deteriorating situation. In the meantime, there was the accompanying pressure of college. It was all too much for this young man to handle. He felt as if he were falling apart, had no control over his life, his very existence terribly threatened. It was as if the end were coming, and there was nothing that he could do about it.

Persons at times like this respond in many different ways, but the purpose is always the attempt to maintain one's existence as a human being, to protect oneself, to discover some meaning in the events. Not experiencing the resources within themselves, and no longer feeling able to cope, many people naturally look to external sources: other people, institutions, God. One method that we all utilized unconsciously to become who we are is the mechanism of identification. We identified with those aspects of our fathers and mothers, and later other people, that we understood at some level as being the source of their strength and power and competence and attractiveness. Even as adults, and especially under great stress, there is the tendency to identify with whatever or whomever seems to be a source of strength.

In addition, every religion has always had as at least part of its power to its adherents some amount of identification with the deity or deities and special figures within the religion's tradition. Identification with Christ has been a part of the Christian faith. This is conceived of and expressed in a number of different ways, such as being a part of the Body of Christ, the church, the eating and drinking of the Sacrament of the Lord's Supper, mystical experience, "the imitation of Christ," and others. Our purpose here is not to go into these into any detail, but merely to remark on the reality of who it is we are in terms of the inevitability of the mechanism of identification and the encouragement of our tradition toward identification with God or Christ, outstanding biblical figures or other great people in the tradition, or, in some faith groups, the saints. This type of identification is a very natural reaction and may be a source of real guidance and strength as we function effectively and realistically in our lives as they usually are. However, under the force of unbearable stress, our exaggerated needs lead us into exaggerated behavior, and *over*-identification, or *whole* identification, may take place. John did this. And he "became" a person who was a "natural" for him and his situation: Daniel, thrown into the den of lions, his life threatened, yet preserved by the power of God. This is precisely the way

John was experiencing his deteriorating life. Preservation was exactly what he needed. Since he felt himself powerless over his destiny, God was the power he needed. Daniel, of course, was not only spared, but he was selected to be spared for a special purpose, to be the one who, through his being delivered, and through his prophecy, was to be God's spokesman to the people of Israel. So John, now Daniel, was a specially chosen one of God.

We can understand, of course, with his declaration of his new identity, announcing his own being chosen by God, and preaching in public places concerning the "end of things," his friends and family were sufficiently troubled to take him to a psychiatrist and then to have him admitted to a psychiatric hospital. The total course of treatment there was designed not only to bring him back to a sense of reality concerning who he was and what world he lived in, but to assist him in developing resources he needed to deal effectively with his life.

After his sense of his own identity as John had for the most part returned, he began attending church. Because of his realistic concern with his own religious life, reuniting himself as a young adult with the way he had actually been raised, the psychiatrist asked the hospital chaplain to talk with him a few times about his religious concerns, including his experience of having been Daniel, help him work out a few distortions which were still troubling him, such as still feeling from time to time as if he were "the chosen one of God" in a way different from other persons, and try to determine how the develoment of his religious life might serve as a constructive force in his growth as a person.

The minister began to get to know him by asking him to share what all of this experience had been like for him, taking seriously the pressures he had been under, being realistic about the inevitability of the destructive aspects of his own earlier behavior, understanding his desperate need for some force to sustain him, trying to appreciate what it meant to him to "be" Daniel, what it was like being hospitalized, and discussing some of what he wanted for himself now.

So for three hours or so over a period of three weeks John and the minister talked. John expressed how frustrated he had been at not being able to handle his life better, how guilty he felt over some of the things he had done, how terrifying it had been to lose control over his life and feel as if it were coming to an end, as if he were doomed. When asked what it had meant to him to "be" Daniel, he responded, "It felt safe. It felt as if I had some power. I could predict the future." The minister affirmed how natural it was to need to feel this way under the circumstances of his life, and that he could understand that it had been very important to him to have experienced himself as this special kind of person. In response to the minister's question, "What was it like when you were brought to the hospital?" John replied that he felt as if he were being punished, and still from time to time he felt special, or as if he were being punished, or both.

In order to deal with these remaining fragments of distortion and to provide a new perspective on the experience of "being Daniel" the minister suggested that they both read the whole book of Daniel in the Bible before they met the next time, and that they use that reading as the explicit basis of their discussion. John had read parts of the book previously only within the context of his delusion of being the prophet. Other aspects of his experience were his perceiving a friend of his as being Jesus and having a vision of the catastrophic end of the world, probably a huge atomic bomb as an outcome of the Vietnam war.

As an introduction to discussing the book itself, John and the minister reviewed how it was he projected his own inner conflicts and turmoil, his sense of his own personal world coming to an end, onto the present external world and how he had worked the biblical material into it. It was in this fashion that he had made the biblical events contemporary, so he could "be" Daniel, and the "end" referred to in the book could be the "end of the world," brought on by some contemporary event, and in the midst of all of this he himself could be saved. In that mental exercise, brought about under such pressure that it could be experienced as his reality for himself, he found a sense of worth and importance and strength and self-maintenance. As all of this was discussed, he began to understand the preservative mechanism of his own mind more clearly than before.

In order to provide a foundation for further clarity for understanding the book, with a view to its contributing a positive contemporary meaning for his life now, the minister then discussed with John the historical situation which formed the setting for its writing, namely the second century B.C., and the existence of the Jewish people in areas where the influence of the Greek language, culture, and religion had been established originally by Alexander the Great.[3] There was a natural pull toward the assimilation of the Jews into the larger cultural context. Obviously, a number of Jews saw such Hellenization as a potential threat to their uniqueness as the people of Jahweh, and their own customs and language were seen as related in an important way to their worship. Therefore, to give up their customs and their language was seen as a force which could diminish their loyalty to God and make their worship less meaningful. Over the years, Palestine was ruled by a number of other countries. In the reign of Antiochus Epiphanes, a Syrian ruler, beginning in 175

B.C., the conflict within the Jewish community and between some of the Jews and the King increased. The King himself showed little respect for the faith of the Jews, and as retribution against the Jews' resistance plundered their temple. The Jews reacted, and the result was a strenuous suppression by the government of Jewish worship, which then gave rise to the Maccabean revolt. After some early military successes, serious and realistic questions began to arise in the minds of a number of Jews concerning the possibility of their victory against the mighty forces of the King. And yet, in the face of such overwhelming odds which threatened their very existence, were they not still called upon to be absolutely faithful to their God? And would he not ultimately, in spite of the realistic assessment of the political and military situation, reestablish his people who were faithful to him?

This, then, was the message of the book of Daniel to the people of God in the particular stories which the book presents. Do not adopt the practices of the foreign people who rule over you. Be faithful to Yahweh. Have courage in the face of overwhelming odds. Your God will save you and establish you as a people. The end of the reign of this foreign king will come, and you will have your opportunity. Yahweh is your future. He will bring you safely through your trials.

Here was the real historical situation, one which is thoroughly understandable. It is also understandable that a book giving the accounts which Daniel does would speak forcefully to many of the Jews of that time. John thoroughly appreciated this situation as he and the minister talked, and the discussion had the force of revelation for him as he understood the meaning and purpose of that book for the people for whom it was originally written. It was not for him alone. The distortion which the biblical material had provided for his particular use and the magical nature of the power he had felt diminished with this cognitive understanding.

At this point the two of them were able to reinterpret the material for John's present benefit. In some ways did his situation not parallel that of the Jews in the second century B.C.? Was not his life being threatened? Was he not facing overwhelming odds? Had there not been temptations to give up his faith as he had known it and depend upon distortions of the faith? Was he not engaged in the struggle to regain his rightful autonomy over his own life? Did he not still need God's help and the help of the community of faith in accomplishing this task? Would not the end of this present age, this reign of a "foreign government" (first, the power of the illness and then the originally experienced "oppression and punishment" of the psychiatric hospital) come to an end in his own life?

The present, existential meaning of the book of Daniel to John is essentially the same: be faithful to your God, worship him, be courageous in the tasks set before you, and be open to his strength. If you persevere to the "end" (not the cataclysmic end of the world, but of the power of this disorder) you will be reestablished as a person in relationship with those whom you love. Again, this message carried for John the force of new revelation, reinforcement for the renewal of his Christian commitment in the realistic context of his own present life, and the renewal of his hope for a worthwhile future.

Using the Bible for Personal Growth

Pastoral care is not only "helping people with problems," it is also doing those concrete acts which intelligent and perceptive Christian love calls us to do. Healing in some form is certainly a major and necessary part of our caring response. But so also are preparations for life's situational and developmental crises, and teaching people how to celebrate God's gifts and life's joys and landmark events. The Bible may be central in these approaches to pastoral care also.

Most of this chapter has obviously been "problem-centered." There need be no apology for this. Most of us welcome any assistance we can get that will make our work with people in critical situations more effective. However, it is also important to reemphasize the "other side" of pastoral care, which is, in the context of this chapter, the use of the Bible to facilitate insight into one's own being as a person, elicit appropriate emotional expression, provide us with a point of identification with biblical writers or figures and with one another in the church today, stimulate faith, and assist movement toward personal growth in any of its dimensions.

Persons may be taught, individually or in groups, to read selected passages in the Bible imaginatively and in such a manner that in a sense they move back into biblical times and into the life situation of the writer or the person being described, and then move again into their own present life-situation, accompanied by the particular Word they have received from their experience. Wink states, "(The text's) capacity for evocation depends upon its resonance with psychic and sociological realities within or impinging upon me. It is therefore legitimate to introject the characters in the Gospel story as probes into one's own self-understanding."[4] The master guide for me in using the Bible for these purposes has been Dr. W. J. A. Power, Professor of Old Testment at Perkins School of Theology, who has very skillfully led several groups of students in this form of reflective, meditative reading and discussion. As some procedures are discussed here, his own unique and helpful contributions are apparent, but he should not be held responsible for what I have added and subtracted. This approach is very similar to that which is referred to and described briefly by Wink, based upon the work of Dr. Elizabeth B. Howes of the Guild for Psychological Studies.[5]

We have already made reference to the fact that the Bible includes the whole gamut of human emotions, behavior, attitudes, experiences, and that we today in our need, to the extent that biblical material is available to us, may use biblical stories, statements, and symbols to express and, in a variety of ways, attempt to meet our needs. Recognizing this, in approaching the Bible with an openness to hearing a Word spoken to us in the midst of our reflection upon a particular passage, the Bible carries a special power to us in our life-situations, whatever they may be. Oates says, "The Bible is the pastor's 'royal road' to the deeper levels of the personalities of his people."[6] It is the road to the deeper levels of the minister's own personality as well, and offers the pastor an opportunity to teach people both in individual pastoral care and counseling or in specially organized groups to walk this road themselves. Consider the following approach:

1. Get physically comfortable.
2. Relax as much as possible. Consciously allow each muscle—limb by limb, section by section of body, if necessary—to relax. Another aid is deliberately to tense each muscle, then let it relax. Take three deep breaths, and relax.
3. Dismiss from the mind as far as possible the immediate conscious pressures and activities of the day by getting some image in your mind: the cross, or Jesus on the cross, or some other Christian symbol. Repeat several times some simple Bible verse, such as, "The Lord is my shepherd."

Now you are ready to read through some preselected passage of scripture, such as Psalm 22, which describes the experience of feeling abandoned by God, or the following: Psalms 18, 31, 32, 42, 73, 103, 137, 138, and 142 (which cry out about suffering and despair); Psalms 17 and 25 (which reveal the writer's sense of being surrounded by enemies); Psalms 40 and 59 (which describe some great positive change that has come about in the writer's life); Psalms 16 and 23 (which express satisfaction and joy); Psalms 35 and 137 (which vent the writer's wrath and desire for revenge and justification); Psalms 90 and 103 (which describe the existential reality of human mortality). Any pastor, of course, can choose many other very appropriate psalms or passages from Jonah (2:2-9), Jeremiah, Isaiah, and others.

First, the person, is asked to read through the entire psalm or other passage, underlining whatever verses seem particularly to strike home personally. Next, reflect on the experiences or thoughts or feelings which are stimulated. If the exercise is being done in a group, members may be paired to discuss with one another their reactions, how certain words in the Bible triggered these reactions, and then later perhaps share some of this with the entire group.

In addition, the pastor might raise with the individual or the group a series of questions, like the following:

"If you had been writing Psalm 31, what would you be describing about yourself? What has it been like, being caught in a 'net'? When you write, 'I am in trouble: my eye is consumed with grief,' what are you expressing? What does it feel like? Let yourself get all the way into the experience and feel it. Reflect on the terror when 'fear was on every side.' " And for other Psalms, "What does it feel like when *your* spirit is faint, when you are in the pit, when it feels as if you are surrounded by your enemies, as if you had been deserted by God?" Or for Psalm 35, "Have you ever felt so angry that you wanted destruction to come upon your enemies, and you wanted to be justified in their eyes and in the eyes of others? What was the experience like? What do you think God's response to this type of anger is?"

These passages, and many more, paint our own humanity on the canvas before our eyes so that we cannot deny who we are, either to ourselves or to each other. But the Bible also makes it clear that this portrait of ourselves is one of many other human portraits, that we participate in a *common* humanity, and that all the pictures are held up by the loving and powerful hands of God himself.

For this use of the Bible to offer the greatest rewards to us and to our individual meditative and reflective reading, raising questions and responding to them, following this type of procedure with another person or with a group may be extremely useful. Sufficient time needs to be allowed for reflecting, thinking, feeling, and being open to one another and to God.

A somewhat different procedure may be used with narrative sections of the Bible, including parables of Jesus which are told in narrative form. An approach to these passages would be to fantasize our being present at that time and in that place for that event. What would we be seeing, hearing, smelling, feeling? Where would we be in the scene? With whom would we identify? What feelings would we be having? Once again, we spend time with each of these, experiencing it, and then, with another person or in a group, sharing with one another where it is we have been experientially.

One psychiatric writing discusses how emotions may be stirred by religious ritual. Some of these may be what is referred to as "regressive" in nature. That is, the verbal and other symbols tap levels of our unconscious, forgotten, or denied experiences and feelings, and then facilitate growth by bringing these into awareness.

Ritual, though, also assists constructive growth by controlling such regression in the provision of form and limits the length of time and the intensity.[7] Using the Bible in ways that we have been describing in this section has the potential of accomplishing some of the same purposes: emotional catharsis, personal insight, and, when with another person or in a group, deepening relationships and developing new interpersonal skills, with the growth being supported and directed by the others with whom we are sharing this experience and by the God who is active in speaking his Word to us. "Insight and feeling coalesce in a story we are striving to tell. When it *becomes* our story—that is, when feeling and insight merge in the symbolic matrix of our being—then the insight furthers the self-formative process."[8]

Summary

This chapter has sought to illustrate how people's references to the Bible reflect something of the significant issues concerning their own lives, and how assisting in a responsible exegesis of the scripture in the context of detailed personal discussion can clarify such issues, make more concrete the questions that are only vaguely formed, and can point the way to resolution. The biblical material can be utilized both to stimulate our feelings, give perspective on our emotional life, affirm the basic goodness of the emotions *as such* as God's gifts to us, and can offer guidelines for more responsible ways of emotional expression. Responsible exegesis can also help people reduce the distortions in their thinking which have been produced through some combination of the intensity of their personal needs and their misuse of the Bible and its symbols, and give to these persons a method of dealing with future problems and crises when they arise and offer a helpful procedure in using the Bible to discover God's will for their lives. This is the process of the Bible's becoming truly *our* story, and when it does this, it also is truly the transforming Word of God to us.

Epilogue: Approaches to a Practical Theology

Pastoral theology may have several starting points. For those of us who are ordained, one very appropriate way to begin is with the question: Who am I as a minister? We ministers are in a profession, a vocation, where, by the very nature of the unity of our faith and calling and what we must necessarily do as a part of our work, we are constantly forced to deal with ourselves as persons and with other persons in a variety of individual and group settings. We must listen and speak, we must be subjective and objective at the same time, and as mortal human beings with our own combination of assets and liabilities, our own aspirations and conflicts and needs, minister to persons in all types of situations and conditions of stress and distress, trouble and extremity. How can we do this?

In addition, we must necessarily ask other questions. Although people may attend a worship service with the self-conscious intent to worship, we cannot escape the fact that preaching is a necessary part of the drama, and a part that is significantly different from the other acts (except that of a pastoral prayer) in that this act is *self*-expressive as the means of proclaiming the gospel: my interpretations, experiences, store of knowledge, styles of speech, and manner of delivery. What characteristics of mine would lead people to be well-served to worship at a service in which I am preaching? Further, what characteristics of mine would lead people to be well-served to come to me (or to receive me) as a Christian pastor?

Pastoral theology must also deal with the meaning of the authority of the office, not as authority inherent in the office itself, but existentially. What authority does *this* person at *this* time attribute to me in *my* office as an ordained minister? Pastoral theology must deal with how we as persons and parsons interpret and utilize this authority in preaching, organizing, educating, and helping.

This book has attempted to speak a few words to these central questions of our existence as ministers. It has not even tried to suggest, except in a few instances by passing references, the many other possible ways of framing some answers: our own prayer and devotional life, our need for worship apart from that which we lead and during which we preach, colleague support groups, or some other gathering of persons who are not ministers, consultation services by other professionals, continuing education programs, et cetera.

Rather, it has sought by means of a particular methodology to support ways of thinking and feeling about ourselves as persons and professionals, to describe the quality of life of the congregation we serve and of which we are also a vital part, and to propose an approach to preaching and the use of the Bible in pastoral care, which, taken together, both improve our effectiveness and have the impact of identifying with clarity our own needs and at some level actively fulfilling these needs in constructive, continually growth-producing ways.

The whole endeavor has been one form of practical theology, of which the issues of pastoral theology just mentioned are a part. Practical theology is a term that has been running around for a long time in search of a definition. It has in fact found many, but there does not yet seem to be anything like a consensus. As it has been actually "performed," it has tended toward one or the other extreme: the application of some biblical and/or historical and systematic theologies to the examination of the underlying motivations and guidelines for functions of ministry and aspects of the life of the community of faith or, on the other hand, merely a label for the collection of the various functions of ministry. The former is quite valid, but only a part of the whole. The latter, taken "as is," is patently inadequate, even false.

The most adequate definitions of practical theology, even when they vary, seem to relate *both* to the theological examination of the forms and practice of the life of the church and its ministry, including the underlying motivations, as well as to how the actual experiences of congregational life and the performance of the functions of the congregation's ministry, including the presence and operation of the ordained minister, may produce a knowledge of the nature of Christian life which feeds back into the initial theological task in a critical, sharpening, and enlightening manner. It is, then, a particular kind of dialectical or continual feedback process, moving from interpretive and systematic thinking about the life of faith and its concerns into the life of the congregation, where experience produces knowledge which then goes back into the interpretive and systematic thinking about the life of faith.

However, I would like to make a suggestion concerning an additional element in a full meaning of the term practical theology. It is what might be called "interdisciplinary correlation." It has just been made clear that practical theology must take the data of human experience with the utmost seriousness, with the source of that experience being the actual life of the congregation and its ministry, the doing of specific functions of ministry. Yet it is also quite clear that we who are the church and who are its ministers, ordained and unordained, also hold membership in a larger world, and we are also informed in our thinking and behavior by this larger world even *as* we are the church and *as* we are performing ministry. When we are informed by the physical sciences, methods of historical criticism, secular literature, philosophy, the social sciences, et cetera, we still act as Christians. Therefore, the contribution of these disciplines to us are also a part of our experience as a church, and it would seem that particular methods of adapting the insights and procedures of these fields in a self-conscious and critical way to our life as a church and to our functions of ministry—to assist both our theological thinking about ministry *and* to increase the quality of our life together and therefore, the effectiveness of ministry—is also practical theology.

It is the attempt to demonstrate something of *this* specific procedure that comprises the basic "theme" of this book. This exercise has sought to make three possible contributions.

First, it demonstrates that practical theology is not a body of "theological knowledge," but a process, a method.

Second, the demonstration of the method might lead ministers to be very self-conscious in the increased use of insights and procedures from other fields for building the life of the church and assisting the functions of ministry in a way that *does not merely borrow* these other disciplines, but which first critiques them theologically and then brings them integrally *into* our theological processes.

Third, the result of this process, as contained in this book, does have a content, namely, suggestions for looking at ourselves, our congregations, and two of our major functions, preaching and pastoral care. Some of this content may very well be brought into the minister's life and work and tested as to its value, to the end that we become better and more effective persons, pastors, and professionals.

Notes

Chapter I

1. Heije Faber, *Pastoral Care in the Modern Hospital* (Philadelphia: The Westminster Press, 1971).
2. Erik H. Erikson, "Growth and Crisis of the 'Healthy Personality.' " In C. Kluckhohn and H. A. Murray (eds.), *Personality in Nature, Society, and Culture,* 2nd ed. (New York: A. A. Knopf, 1965), p. 218.
3. David Switzer, *The Minister as Crisis Counselor* (Nashville: Abingdon, 1974), pp. 21-24.
4. Paul Tillich, *Dynamics of Faith* (New York: Harper, 1957), p. 41.
5. *Ibid.,* pp. 41-43.
6. Faber, *Pastoral Care,* p. 83.
7. Robert R. Carkhuff, *Helping and Human Relations,* 2 vols. (New York: Holt, Rinehart & Winston, 1969), II, 7.
8. Carkhuff, *Helping,* vol. I, 45.
9. *Ibid.,* pp. xi-xiv.
10. *Ibid.,* p. xii.
11. *Ibid.,* p. xiv.
12. *Ibid.,* p. 45.
13. William A. Clebsch, and Charles R. Jaekle, *Pastoral Care in Historical Perspective* (Englewood Cliffs, N.J.: Prentice-Hall, 1964), pp. 8-9.
14. James Glasse, *Profession: Minister* (Nashville: Abingdon, 1968), p. 38.
15. Carkhuff, *Helping,* vol. I, 259.

Chapter II

1. Paul Minear, *Images of the Church and the New Testament* (Philadelphia: The Westminster Press, 1960), p. 166.
2. Johannes Pederson, *Israel,* vol. 1 (London: Oxford University Press, 1926), p. 49.
3. *Ibid,* p. 44.
4. Minear, *Images of the Church,* p. 167.
5. W. Robert Beavers, "The Application of Family Systems Theory to Crisis Intervention," in David K. Switzer, *The Minister as Crisis Counselor* (Nashville: Abingdon, 1974), pp. 181-210. For a more detailed and technical discussion, along with a list of references, see W. Robert Beavers, "A Theoretical Basis for Family Evaluation," in Jerry Lewis, W. Robert Beavers, John T. Gossett, and Virginia Austin Phillips, *No Single Thread* (New York: Bruner/Mazel, 1976), pp. 46-82.
6. Lewis et al., *No Single Thread.*
7. *Ibid.,* pp. 100-101.
8. *Ibid.,* p. 206.
9. *Ibid.,* p. 101.
10. *Ibid.,* p. 102.

11. *Ibid.,* pp. 103-4, 208-9.
12. *Ibid.,* pp. 101-2.
13. *Ibid.,* p. 213.
14. *Ibid.,* p. 212.

Chapter III

1. Paul Tillich, *Systematic Theology,* vol. I (University of Chicago Press, 1951), pp. 59 ff.
2. James T. Cleland, *Preaching to Be Understood* (Nashville: Abingdon Press, 1965) pp. 33 ff.
3. *Ibid.,* p. 43.
4. Arthur L. Teikmanis, *Preaching and Pastoral Care* (Englewood Cliffs, N.J.: Prentice-Hall, 1964). p. 19.
5. Rodney Hunter, "Ministry-or Magic?" *Candler Review* (May 1976), p. 13.
6. *Ibid.,* pp. 12, 14-15.
7. David K. Switzer, *The Dynamics of Grief* (Nashville: Abingdon, 1970), pp. 81-91.
8. Mary Daly, *Beyond God the Father: Toward a Philosopy of Women's Liberation* (Boston: Beacon Press, 1973), pp. 33-34.
9. Gerhard Ebeling, *Word and Faith* (London: S.C.M. Press, 1963), p. 324.
10. *Ibid.,* p. 325.
11. *Ibid.,* p. 186.
12. S. I. Hayakawa, *Language in Thought and Action* (New York: Harcourt, Brace, 1949), p. 186.
13. Ebeling, *Word and Faith,* p. 190.
14. Phillips Brooks, *Lectures on Preaching* (New York: E.P. Dutton, 1877), p. 5.
15. Hunter, "Ministry-or Magic?" p. 14.
16. Martin Buber, *I-Thou* (2nd ed.) (New York: Charles Scribner's Sons, 1958), pp. 3, 12, 33, 40-41.
17. *Ibid.,* pp. 3, 11, 33, 63.
18. *Ibid.,* p. 75-76
19. Carkhuff, *Helping,* vols. I and II.
20. Switzer, *The Minister as Crisis Counselor,* pp. 72-77.

Chapter IV

1. Carkhuff, vol. II, pp. 5, 7-8.
2. Carl Rogers, *On Becoming a Person* (Boston: Houghton Mifflin Co., 1961), pp. 61-63, 282-84.
3. Carkhuff, *Helping,* vol. I, pp. 173-77.
4. Edgar N. Jackson, *Psychology of Preaching* (New York: Channel Press, 1961) p. 64.
5. Harry Emerson Fosdick, "What Is the Matter with Preaching?" *Preaching,* II, 1 (1967), p. 5.

6. O. C. Edwards, *The Living and Active Word* (New York: Seabury Press 1975).
7. Carkhuff, *Helping,* vol. I, pp. 178-81.
8. W. Robert Beavers, *Psychotherapy and Growth* (New York: Bruner/Mazel, 1977), pp. 317-22.
9. Unpublished manuscript.
10. Carkhuff, *Helping,* vol. I, pp. 181-84.
11. Fosdick, "What Is the Matter?" pp. 7-8.
12. Earl H. Ferguson, "Abstractions in Preaching," *Pastoral Psychology,* XIV, 137 (October 1963), p. 8.
13. Charles F. Kemp, *Pastoral Preaching* (St. Louis, Bethany Press, 1963), p. 24.
14. Carkhuff, *Helping,* vol. I, pp. 184-87.
15. *Ibid.,* pp. 187-89.
16. *Ibid.,* pp. 189-91.
17. Howard Clinebell, *Basic Types of Pastoral Counseling* (Nashville: Abingdon, 1966), p. 227.
18. Carkhuff, *Helping,* vol. I, pp. 192-95.

Chapter V

1. Theodore Reik, *Listening with the Third Ear* (New York: Farrar, Straus, 1948), p. 144.
2. Doyle I. Carson and Jerry M. Lewis, "Ocular auto-enucleation while under the influence of drugs: A case report." *Adolescence,* VI, 23 (1971) pp. 398-99.
3. The material in this paragraph is drawn from Arthur Jeffrey, "The Book of Daniel," *The Interpreter's Bible,* Vol. 6 (Nashville: Abingdon Press, 1956), pp. 341 ff.
4. Walter Wink, *The Bible in Human Transformation* (Philadelphia: Fortress Press, 1973), p. 55.
5. *Ibid.,* pp. 49-68.
6. Wayne Oates, *The Bible and Pastoral Care.* (Philadelphia: The Westminster Press, 1953), p. 21.
7. Group for the Advancement of Psychiatry, *The Psychic Functions of Religion in Mental Illness and Health,* No. 67 (New York: Mental Health Materials Center, 1968) pp. 703-4.
8. Wink, *Human Transformation,* p. 63.

CEDS LIBRARY

32112936